A Writing Center Practitioner's Inquiry into Collaboration

This book presents a model of Practitioner Inquiry (PI) as a systematic form of empirical research and provides a rationale for its suitability within a writing center context. Exploring the potential of writing centers as pedagogical sites that support research, the book offers an accessible model that guides both research and practice for writing center practitioners, while offering flexibility to account for their distinct contexts of practice.

Responding to the increasing call in the field to produce empirical "RAD" (replicable, aggregable, data-driven) research, the author explores Practitioner Inquiry through explication of methodology and methods, a revisitation of collaboration to guide both practice and research, and examples of application of the model. Nordstrom grounds this research and scholarship in Hawaiʻi's context and explores Indigenous concepts and approaches to inform an ethical collaborative practice.

Offering significant contributions to empirical research in the fields of writing center studies, composition, and education, this book will be of great relevance to writing center practitioners, anyone conducting empirical research, and researchers working in tutor professionalization, collaboration, translingual literacy practices, and research methodologies.

Georganne Nordstrom is an Associate Professor and Associate Chair of the English Department at the University of Hawaiʻi at Mānoa. Her research and teaching focus on writing center studies, critical place-based pedagogy, and Indigenous and minority rhetorics. A 2018–19 Fulbright Scholar, Dr. Nordstrom is also the recipient of the 2012 Richard Braddock Award and is Vice President of the International Writing Center Organization.

Routledge Research in Writing Studies

Digital Reading and Writing in Composition Studies
Edited by Mary R. Lamb and Jennifer Parrott

Writing Democracy
Taking the Political Turn In and Beyond The Trump Era
Edited by Shannon Carter, Deborah Mutnick, Stephen Parks, and Jessica Pauszek

Writing Centers at the Center of Change
Edited by Joe Essid & Brian McTague

Teaching Writing, Rhetoric, and Reason at the Globalizing University
Robert Samuels

Arts-Based Research Methods in Writing Studies
A Primer
Kate Hanzalik

A Writing Center Practitioner's Inquiry into Collaboration
Pedagogy, Practice, And Research
Georganne Nordstrom

Engaging Research Communities in Writing Studies
Ethics, Public Policy, and Research Design
Johanna L. Phelps

For more information about this series, please visit: https://www.routledge.com

A Writing Center Practitioner's Inquiry into Collaboration
Pedagogy, Practice, And Research

Georganne Nordstrom

NEW YORK AND LONDON

First published 2021
by Routledge
52 Vanderbilt Avenue, New York, NY 10017

and by Routledge
2 Park Square, Milton Park, Abingdon, Oxon, OX14 4RN

Routledge is an imprint of the Taylor & Francis Group, an informa business

© 2021 Georganne Nordstrom

The right of Georganne Nordstrom to be identified as author of this work has been asserted by her in accordance with sections 77 and 78 of the Copyright, Designs and Patents Act 1988.

All rights reserved. No part of this book may be reprinted or reproduced or utilised in any form or by any electronic, mechanical, or other means, now known or hereafter invented, including photocopying and recording, or in any information storage or retrieval system, without permission in writing from the publishers.

Trademark notice: Product or corporate names may be trademarks or registered trademarks, and are used only for identification and explanation without intent to infringe.

Library of Congress Cataloging-in-Publication Data
A catalog record for this title has been requested

ISBN: 978-0-367-51025-1 (hbk)
ISBN: 978-1-003-05214-2 (ebk)

Typeset in Times New Roman
by codeMantra

This book is dedicated to the
UHM Writing Center Consultants 2012–2020

Contents

Figure ix
List of Tables xi
Acknowledgments xiii

Introduction: Practitioner Inquiry and
Empirical Research in the Writing Center 1

1 What Indigenous Practices Can Teach Us about
Collaboration 25

2 Practitioner Inquiry: A Model for Research and
Practice in the Writing Center 55

3 A Practitioner's Inquiry into Tutor
Professionalization *vis-à-vis* Collaboration 75

4 Translingual Practices vs. Academic Discourse:
Writing Center Consultants Weigh in on
Supporting Writers' Multiliteracy Repertoires 98

Epilogue: A Practitioner's Final Thoughts 119

Index 123

Figure

2.1 Practitioner Inquiry Research Model 70

Tables

2.1 Comparison of Practitioner Inquiry Models from
    Education and Writing Center Studies 58
3.1 Summary of Number of Evaluation Responses
    for Each Question 88
3.2 In Vivo Groupings 90
3.3 Comparison of Singular to Collective Pronoun Usage 93
4.1 Distribution of Data Points across Themes by Cohort 109

Acknowledgments

I must first acknowledge the ʻāina where I have lived and learned—Kahaluʻu, Kailua, and Kaʻaʻawa—and the many kumu and hoa aloha who have so generously welcomed me and shared their ʻike, manaʻo, and aloha. I hope this project honors all that you have given me.

The following two articles are reprinted in this volume in revised form: "Practitioner Inquiry: Articulating a Model for RAD Research in the Writing Center" (*The Writing Center Journal* (2015), *35*(1), 87–116)); and "A Practitioner's Inquiry into Professionalization: When *We* does not Equal Collaboration" (*Praxis: A Writing Center Journal, 17*(1)).

To all the University of Hawaiʻi at Mānoa Writing Center consultants with whom I have had the privilege and honor of working with since 2012, many of whom participated in the studies presented in Chapters 3 and 4—you have been a constant inspiration. Mahalo piha. You are inscribed on every page of this book.

I am grateful to the many mentors who have provided models of excellence and helped shape me into the practitioner I am, including Jim Henry, Cristina Bacchilega, Jeff Carroll, Craig Howes, Laura Lyons, and Glenn Man. Mahalo nui Brandy Nālani McDougall, kuʻualoha hoʻomanawanui, and Sherry Wynn Perdue. Through my collaborations with each of you, I have learned so much, and I am so very grateful for your friendship, feedback, and support throughout this project. I have also benefited in countless ways from the intellectual richness and collegiality of my colleagues at the University of Hawaiʻi, in particular, thank you Sarah Allen, Derrick Higginbotham, Anna Feuerstein, Jack Taylor, John Zuern, David Stannard, Candace Fujikane, and Subramanian Shankar.

I am also very grateful to the Fulbright Scholar Program for the 2019 award that made it possible for me to work and research in Ireland, and to all those in the English Department and James Hardiman

Library at the National University of Ireland Galway (NUIG) who made my stay possible and welcomed me. Ira Ruppo—thank you for answering that first email, and for your generosity and friendship. I am so very proud of our collaborations. And a special shout out to the consultants from NUIG's Academic Writing Centre for sharing their time and knowledge with me while I was there, and particularly for their input on the study presented in Chapter 4.

My thanks to Suzanne Richardson and the editorial team at Taylor and Francis/Routledge for their belief and interest in this project as well as their guidance throughout the process.

My inner circle: my family—my mom, Dolores Minton, my sisters and brother, cousins, and nieces and nephews—they may not always know exactly what I am up to, but they always have my back anyway. I got you folks too. Pi'ikea, we have been in lockstep for 40+, and I cannot imagine it any other way. Mahalo my sister for being there throughout. And, my ultimate inspiration, Keanu and Kea, thank you for always reminding me what is most important.

Finally, to my partner in everything, Hervé—I am so grateful for your constant love and support. Thank you for always making the journey so much better.

Introduction
Practitioner Inquiry and Empirical Research in the Writing Center

> Writing centers are pedagogical sites that support writing and research.

That is my mantra. I repeat it in staff meetings, in meetings with campus administrators, it even begins our mission statement. It reflects my understanding of writing center practice as a multitiered cyclical endeavor, with practitioners engaging in research into the many factors that go into administering our services so as to refine our pedagogy for training and professionalizing our consultants[1] and to inform the work we do with writers. At each juncture, this work is infused with the goal to support every writer by cultivating an educational space where diverse voices—both consultants' and writers' who visit the center—can exercise their right to agency. Understanding our spaces as liminal (Denny, 2010) is apropos, as it is through this positioning that we are able to interrogate and counter the hierarchical structures within our institutions, which, in turn, engenders access for our consultants, the writers they work with, as well as for the centers themselves and their administrators. Drawing on queer theory to conceptualize the liminality of writing centers, Harry Denny explicates how it informs a pedagogical approach that nurtures critical engagement and issues of access:

> This sort of borderland practice underscores a transitory, fluid existence that disrupts the polarity of margin and center, forcing one to bleed into the other. Even better, in writing centers, these contact zones champion discursive complication and the (de)mystification of process, rhetoric, and audience. A subversive, even queer, writing center practice turns on tutors and clients alike coming to recognize the arbitrary nature of the dominant,

enabling both to make strategic decisions to play along or to create cogent responses should they choose to resist or further challenge and question.

(p. 110)

Many of us in the field embrace our liminality, acknowledging all we can accomplish from this transformative space; however, misconceptions about writing centers as fix-it shops or markers of academic inferiority for those who visit (like those outlined by Stephen North's (1984a) germinal essay), while not as pervasive, still persist. While our liminality promotes inclusivity—a concept recently gaining traction but really an ideal that has always been foundational to our work—this institutional positioning can also compromise our agency over our work, the discourse surrounding that work, and ultimately who we work with and how we are able to work. It is through research, specifically empirical research, that we can legitimate that liminality within the institution. For me, this vision of writing centers as spaces where research, practice, and theory are simultaneously engaged is the essence of my stance as a writing center practitioner; it informs how I approach and enact my work. This project is born out of my commitment to realize the potential of writing centers as pedagogical sites that support writing and research. It embodies how I see these projects—fostering a rigorous learning environment, supporting inclusion and access in practice, and conducting ethical empirical research—as one mission. The practice and research framework I present is designed to bring these projects together within one cohesive model.

Before proceeding, it is useful here to define several terms I use throughout the book and clarify the relationship between methodology, method, research model, and research design. First, following a precedent set by others in the field (North, 1984b; Gillespie et al., 2002; Babcock & Thonus, 2012; Grutsch McKinney, 2015), I use *research* to refer to empirical investigation and *scholarship* to refer to conceptual inquiry. I do not privilege one over the other, as I hold they both play important roles in our work, which, I hope, is evident in the model I present. As for *methodology* and *method*, I work from Sandra Harding's (1987) explanation that methodology "is a theory and analysis of how research does or should proceed" (p. 3), whereas method "is a technique for (or way of proceeding in) gathering evidence" (p. 2). A methodology is informed by theories that represent foundational tenets, values, and ethical concerns. In writing center studies, collaboration would be a foundational tenet that encompasses values and ethical concerns of practitioners in the field. A methodology also encompasses certain approaches, such as validity and systematicity, meant to realize those same interests in research design and when working with data. Methods, on the other hand, refer to practices enacted in the process of research and should be designed so as to support the claims of the methodology. For example, conducting a case study, performing extensive review of the literature, or administering surveys are all possible methods. The specific practices enacted as part of any method—how data are gathered and documented, the way the researcher's relationship to the research participants or subject is defined, how the research and participants are represented, and so forth—must be informed by the methodology. Finally, it is *research model* that refers to the conceptual framework that encompasses both methodology and methods, indicating how methodology should inform particular methods at various points in the research process. Importantly, a model also suggests sequencing in terms of how research should proceed in a very general sense from inception through analysis and presentation of outcomes.[2] A research model outlines the possible parameters to broadly address the concerns of a research context in general terms, whereas a *research design* specifies those parameters and approaches as they are applied in a particular study.

This project is about determining a methodology to guide both our practices and research in ways that support our foundational tenets, such as collaboration, and at the same time account for the uniqueness of our individual contexts. It is about foregrounding traits prized in writing center studies, such as ensuring our practices are ethical and support inclusivity. As most writing center practitioners recognize, the literal places of our centers have profound impact on not only who we work with but how we work, and not just at the institutional level; our wider communities too must be taken into account. In my case, I live and work in Hawaiʻi, a place where the negative effects of colonization on education and access are all too evident. I grew up hearing the egregious claims that quiet, non-white students are disengaged, with the individuals who perpetuate such damaging rhetoric—often teachers—intentionally ignoring the obvious fact that the ways students interact in a classroom are often informed by sociocultural norms and do not reflect intellectual superiority or inferiority. I have also witnessed these kinds of sedimented stereotypes inhibit students' chances of success. I know only too well how reading an observation within a certain bias can elicit problematic interpretations that are too often flat out wrong. The majority of students my writing center employs and provides a service to identify with groups that have at one point or another been marginalized and disenfranchised—they are mostly people of color. Many of their histories and experiences have been misrepresented, and most have been on the receiving end of negative and misinformed stereotypes, especially in terms of literacy practices and academic preparedness. All of us have, at one point or another, confronted "research" that misrepresents lived realities by reading data through a lens that privileges Western norms or failing to take into account variables that could render outcomes incomplete or inaccurate. All these factors played a significant role as I articulated the model presented in the ensuing chapters.

Since my undergraduate days I have been drawn to empirical research as a way to counter harmful (mis)representations and provide a fuller understanding of why some student groups underperform within mainstream academic standards. As a master's student, I undertook an empirical investigation into the variability of students from different language groups making use of our writing center (Nordstrom, 2003). I was specifically concerned with why our local students, many who identify as Pidgin speakers (Hawai'i Creole), were not represented well among our visitors and whether this phenomenon resulted from perceptions that using the writing center is an inferiority marker for them in a way it is not for multilingual speakers from countries outside the U.S. And, when writing my dissertation, I again employed an empirical framework to examine student writing to identify context-specific iterations that demonstrate critical engagement that can be missed by teachers unfamiliar with literacy practices tied to this place. In my work, empirical research has provided an avenue to more fully capture the students I work with, both providing insights into ways pedagogy can be adapted to improve efficacy and to dispel misrepresentations of students from this place as underperforming. Now, as a writing center director, I see empirical investigations as accomplishing all this and more—it also supports my efforts to gain legitimacy without having to conform (too much) to perceptions about what we should be or what we should do.

However, empiricism alone does not fully attend to the concerns that prompted the aforementioned investigations. A guiding methodology that foregrounds issues of representation and inclusivity is essential. While I have long employed Practitioner Inquiry as a framework in my empirical research, Indigenous theories of pedagogy and research have also played an instrumental role in my work. Indigenous theories foreground collaboration, and, as they have been reformulated to counter hundreds of years of violence and disenfranchisement, they identify practices meant to inhibit misappropriation and misrepresentation. Particularly in my context, such practices are essential; however, as I will discuss at length in Chapter 1, with their focus on ethics and inclusivity, I argue that practices informed by Indigenous approaches also work with non-Indigenous students and in a multitude of research contexts because at the very foundation, they promote ethical ways of engaging with students and research participants. With the recent (and growing) attention to empirical research in writing center studies, my investment seems not unique. But what is missing from many of these treatments of empirical research by writing center scholars is a complete explication of a model that includes a methodology to guide this work.

When attempting to articulate a model that is attractive to a whole discipline, it seems the best place to start is with what people are already doing and practices that are already working. Early writing center scholarship provides some clear indicators—it is replete with accounts of observations of writing center occurrences alongside analysis. While such accounts are often cast as a version of ethnographic participant-observation, participant-observation sans rigorous protocols that demand systematicity and triangulation does not result in conclusions that can be verified, much less transferable to other sites, even if one *knows* outcomes are recurring. In other words, noticing an outcome happens repeatedly is not research—it is merely the first step. The early literature in writing center studies provides a plethora of observances that point to our experiences representing predictable outcomes, but without the tools to capture nuances and variables, we are unable to identify precisely how and why certain outcomes manifest—or why a similar scenario produced a different outcome. Although participant-observation remains one of my core practices, when designing my first research project, I quickly realized I needed additional tools to account for multiple variables and explain repeated phenomena; otherwise, attributing factors might be overlooked and outcomes discounted as coincidence. While my observations may make for an interesting read and may even be convincing to other writing center practitioners who have witnessed similar scenarios, stopping research at this point does not broaden our disciplinary discussion beyond *this is what happened at one point in one center*. Because writing center research most often involves people, outcomes can depend largely on an individual's behavior, personal characteristics, etc., not to mention the practitioner's own biases, which may lead to an unintentional skew in interpretation. To balance that kind of variability, methods and analytical approaches need to be concretized as much as possible; otherwise, such inquiry only makes for a good story.

A model that moves from informed speculation to verifiable research would thus need to encompass protocols that attend to issues of documentation and representation, such as:

- How do I explain an outcome so that it is clear and logical to others?
- How do I demonstrate the outcomes are not a one-time occurrence realized by a few students in a unique setting, but rather linked to practices and repeatable across student populations?
- How do I demonstrate I am not "seeing" data in a way that promotes what I am looking for? In other words, how do I demonstrate the evidence I gathered is not overly biased by my own positioning/research intentions?

Even a basic understanding of Practitioner Inquiry points to its applicability to a writing center context: in Practitioner Inquiry, a practitioner conducts research in their site of practice, with observation of practices and interactions playing a key role in inquiry. Unfortunately, however, too often when Practitioner Inquiry has been identified as a study's guiding methodology (in writing center studies, mostly by scholars doing taxonomical work, as it is rarely invoked by the researchers themselves), the inquiry part of the process stops with an anecdotal description of observation. In contrast, scholarship actually defining Practitioner Inquiry reveals it as a robust research model that supports data-based research. For scholars examining Practitioner Inquiry in both education (Cochran-Smith & Lytle, 2009) and writing center studies (Liggett, Jordan, & Price, 2011), it goes beyond a practitioner in an educational setting observing a problem or practice-outcome scenario. Rather, Practitioner Inquiry encompasses theoretical approaches for conducting and documenting research as well as practices for gathering and analyzing data. It emphasizes the role of practice in the research, accounts for a practitioner's stance in approach to research and research subject, and provides a framework for gathering, presenting, and analyzing the data.

Institutionally, however, the concept of "practitioner" carries some baggage, and in terms of research, Practitioner Inquiry has often been trivialized in the academic arena. Arguably its marginalization is in part due to its emergence in response to institutional contexts that devalued teachers in the university's researcher/teacher paradigm that traditionally saw these endeavors as hierarchically separate (which I explain in the next section). Also inhibiting its traction as a viable research model is a lack of general understanding and articulation of what Practitioner Inquiry is and what enacting it entails. Too often it has been used to describe any inquiry conducted by a practitioner-researcher, and, unfortunately, some of this work is not research as it is defined here—it does not foreground the systematic rigor when working with data that is necessary for a study to count as research. This has resulted in Practitioner Inquiry research often being dismissed as informal research. Dana Driscoll & Sherry Wynn Perdue (2012), for example, critique certain kinds of research often included under the Practitioner Inquiry umbrella for its subjectivity and lack of data integrity, writing, "While it is often marketed as research and inhabits a substantial place in *WCJ*, this kind of scholarship offers little more than anecdotal evidence, one person's experience, to support its claim" (p. 16). A closer examination of Practitioner Inquiry models discussed in the literature (i.e., Cochran-Smith & Lytle, 2009; Liggett, Jordan, & Price, 2011), however, implicates responsibility, rigor, and integrity on the part of the practitioner-researcher in approach to methods, data collection, and representation of results. With this project, I hope to intervene in representations of Practitioner Inquiry as lacking rigor, and, aligning with more robust treatments, present it as an accessible and efficacious model that guides both research and practice for practitioners working in writing centers as well as other educational contexts.

Affirming Practitioners as Inquirers

Practitioner Inquiry is a relatively new iteration of Teacher Research, intended to broaden the scope and increase inclusivity in terms of practitioner roles and study contexts previously bound by the modifier "teacher." The Teacher Research movement, largely attributed to the work of Lawrence Stenhouse in England in the 1960s, gained momentum during the 1970s and 1980s in the U.S., and evolved in response to the devaluing of teaching and teachers because of the "false dichotomy" between teaching and research in institutional settings (Ray, 1993, pp. 49–50). Early Teacher Research projects were aimed at countering the perception that teachers were conduits in disseminating knowledge but played no role in creating it or instigating change based on that knowledge. The influential 1987 anthology by Dixie Goswami and Peter Stillman, *Reclaiming the Classroom: Teacher Research as an Agency for Change*, includes essays that explore how and why to conduct Teacher Research, with an overarching argument that it is teachers who should generate theories through collaboration with other teachers and not adhere solely to findings produced through university-based research endeavors.

Corresponding with this effort to redefine the teacher's role, many who embraced the idea of Teacher Research as "agency for change," grounded their projects in critical and democratic social theory to inform examinations of alternative ways of knowing and constructing knowledge. Moreover, they provided the theoretical foundation through which to critique dominant discourse in academic institutions that sanctioned top-down knowledge dissemination (Cochran-Smith & Lytle, 1999b, pp. 15–16). Much of the work during this period was aimed at interrogating and reversing the traditional avenues of knowledge transmission, which, by their very top-down nature, implied the privileging of knowledge tied to certain discourse communities. Teacher Research advocates countered these established institutional practices, arguing that teachers are the instrumental force behind the work of schools. These efforts to emancipate the practitioner so as to improve curriculum (Stenhouse, 1983, p. 1) correlated with those of other teacher researchers committed to progressive education. Marilyn Cochran-Smith and Susan Lytle (1999b) write that these endeavors "emphasized the importance of teachers as expert knowers about their own students and classroom" (p. 16). While these moves worked to reposition teachers as experts, not only over their practice but also in terms of what and how to research, they also highlighted that a wide array of individuals working in other educational contexts were (and still often are) similarly marginalized.

Noting the limitations embodied in the terminology "Teacher Research," scholars such as Cochran-Smith & Lytle (2009) advocated replacing "teacher" with "practitioner." In *Inquiry as Stance: Practitioner Research for the Next Generation*, they assert that "*teacher* unnecessarily and inaccurately narrowed the scope" (p. ix). They then provide *Practitioner Research* and *Practitioner Inquiry* (the latter being the term I employ) as interchangeable terms that encompass Teacher Research but are more "expansive and inclusive" in that they refer to "a wide array of educational practitioners" in addition to teachers (p. ix). In this new construction, Practitioner Inquiry thus becomes an umbrella term that encompasses Teacher Research. The broader parameters of Practitioner Inquiry allow for the adaptation of many of the same Teacher Research practices and approaches, yet also acknowledge that complex, multidirectional relationships occur in other educational settings as well, like, for example, writing centers. Despite the variability in terms of the ways and locations in which Practitioner Inquiry can be applied, there are shared features, such as the practitioner assumes a dual role as researcher; the professional context and professional practice are the focus of inquiry; and the boundaries between practice and inquiry become blurred as research and practice are enacted in the same context, often at the same time, and involving the same individual/s (Cochran-Smith & Lytle, 2009, pp. 41–43).[3] Importantly, collaboration and social construction of knowledge, or the acknowledgment of other's knowledge and expertise as it pertains to their experiences and living and working conditions, are also foundational in all forms of Practitioner Inquiry. These last two elements overtly point to an attitudinal positioning of the practitioner, indicating the prominence of their role in this model.

At the very heart of Practitioner Inquiry are the practitioners, but that begs the question, just who is a practitioner? Obviously, the concept of *practitioner* is rooted in practice—the idea that an individual has or is gaining an expertise in some kind of practice that requires specialized knowledge or skill—and most dictionary definitions associate these skills with a specific profession (dictionary.com; Merriam-Webster.com). Practitioners can be novice, advanced, or even experts—but what distinguishes an individual as a practitioner, though, is arguably tied to their professionalism. Treatments of professionalism (Joseph, 2018; MindTools, 2019) point to commitment and investment in developing and improving one's own expertise to enhance job performance and improve the work environment. Connecting professionalism to practitioner further centralizes the work context and the work that is done there. It also engenders reflection and efforts to improve work and its conditions. Using my own writing center context as example, I consider myself a writing center practitioner, not because of my position as director, but rather because of my commitment to writing center work, my experience working in writing centers, and my ongoing research interests in the field. As for the consultants I work with, many remain in the center for two or more years. They are committed to the work of the center in general and invested in honing their skills. They actively seek out ways to improve their own approaches as well as the general atmosphere of the center. A few have attended and presented at national conferences, and some have published. Several consultants have demonstrated sustained interest and commitment over several years and have focused their milestone projects like thesis and dissertations on writing center studies. I would consider all of these individuals practitioners, albeit to varying degrees in the novice-advanced continuum. One attribute that distinguishes all these practitioners is in how they construct their *stance* in relation to their work.

With the publication of *Inquiry as Stance: Practitioner Research for the Next Generation*, in addition to arguing for more inclusivity through the broadened identifier of practitioner, Cochran-Smith & Lytle (2009) also explain *inquiry as stance* as inherent in Practitioner Inquiry. For Cochran-Smith & Lytle, inquiry as stance represents "a worldview and habit of mind" (p. viii) that prompts the practitioner to continually reflect on practices, with this reflection prompting research when appropriate with the end goal of improving educational outcomes in a specific context (p. 2). In other words, for a practitioner operating within a Practitioner Inquiry framework, their stance creates a lens wherein assessment of the wide-ranging practices and interactions that occur in the site of practice is constant and ongoing, with the possibility of formal investigation always viable. To put it succinctly, for practitioners assuming this stance, every day they inhabit their practice/research site there is a subject for research waiting to be identified. We are always asking ourselves and those we work with the following questions: Why is/isn't something working? How could it work better? What have we failed to consider? Inquiry as stance differs significantly from the process in many paradigms where a research project is conceived and then brought into a context where it will be conducted. Indeed, it is different from the approach taken in many dominant research models that discuss research mostly in terms of methods and strategies but diminish (or ignore) the researcher as a variable. In Practitioner Inquiry, the practitioner shapes the research just as the research has a direct impact on their work. And it is their stance that infuses this work, which points to the need to more closely examine the concept of stance sans the inquiry modifier.

While inquiry as stance is intrinsically connected to Practitioner Inquiry in that it is an element that signifies the practitioner's objective of constantly improving working conditions in the broadest sense, the particulars of how one's stance influences this work is arguably more individualized. One's stance manifests the practitioner's values and the terministic screen that colors their worldview. When Cochran-Smith & Lytle (1999a) first began constructing the concept of inquiry as stance, they worked with the metaphor of how one stands to illustrate what stance embodies:

> We use the metaphor of stance to suggest both orientational and positional ideas, to carry allusions to the physical placing of the body as well as to intellectual activities and perspectives over time. In this sense, the metaphor is intended to capture the ways we stand, the ways we see, and the lenses we see through.
>
> (p. 288)

"Way" and "lens" are the words in this description that I want to further complicate, and for this I look to work in linguistics where the concept of stance has received significant attention.[4] John W. Du Bois (2007) explains stance through articulation of what it achieves: "In taking stance, the stancetaker (1) evaluates an object, (2) positions a subject (usually self), and (3) aligns with other subjects" (163).[5] So, working off of Du Bois's definition, evaluate, position, and align are the key terms impacting one's stance. Each one of these terms indicates a behavior informed subjectively and involving some kind of value judgment informed by an individual's sociocultural grounding, their ideological constructs, their priorities, and their negotiation of contextual exigencies. I return to a writing center context to illustrate how stance thus conceived might manifest *vis-à-vis* inquiry. In writing center studies, inclusivity remains a dominant theme when articulating best practices, and it would not be unusual for a writing center practitioner to be attentive to the extent to which their welcoming practices reach specific demographics of students. Inquiry as stance, as articulated by Cochran Smith & Lytle (2009), points to a writing center practitioner regularly assessing how welcoming practices enacted in their center achieve this objective, which might entail performing an empirical investigation of identified practices followed by data analysis to determine their efficacy; however, it is the practitioner's stance in particular that determines the discreet intersections between practice and student demographic necessitating examination. Moreover, while stance is unquestionably influenced by sociocultural variables, for some, those factors become grounded in theoretical framework, like Queer theory, Feminist theory, or, in my own case, Indigenous theories, and these theoretical groundings influence how we shape our practices to foreground certain values and priorities.

A recent article I coauthored with seven of my consultants (Nordstrom et al., 2019), "Affirming Our Liminality & Writing on the Walls: How We Welcome in Our Writing Center," provides a succinct example of the way our stances influence how we see and shape our practices. My coauthors are all experienced practitioners and include undergraduates, MA students, and PhD candidates. The multimodal article is made up of eight short pieces, one written by each of us describing "how we welcome." The specific topic of each of the pieces differs, with individuals focusing on historicizing our center, enacting a place-based pedagogy, engendering communal writing activities, supporting LBTQIA students, using Universal Design Learning, designing undergraduate generated heuristics, and my own piece on adapting a Kanaka Maoli (Native Hawaiian) practice to diffuse a situation. The varied topics represent, at that point in time, what we each saw as important with regard to "welcoming." Some of us approached welcoming in terms of the student writers we work with, whether through the aesthetics of the space, leisurely activities, or respecting different identities and learning styles. Others viewed welcoming in regard to how we include our new consulting cohorts and create space for them to be experts. Delving into the pieces more substantially reveals different theoretical groundings that also informs these practitioners' stances, coloring the lens through which they approach their subjects. While collectively we all embrace inclusivity, the peculiarities of our stances direct not only how we see shortfalls in terms of inclusivity but also our ideas about how to attend to disparities. The beauty of this piece for me is that it showcases that the people I work with bring new insights and perspectives—their stances differ from mine—and the spirit of collaboration imbued in Practitioner Inquiry embraces these multiple stances so that we can see things we may have missed, recognize different interpretations, and find solutions we did not even entertain as possible.

This example illustrates how stances toward the same topic can manifest differently and captures the wide range of individuals who are practitioners. Indeed, the snippets, although short, reflect inquiry into practices enacted in our site of practice, and thus could be considered a form of Practitioner Inquiry. But, returning to the definitions I began with, this work would fall into the category of conceptual inquiry or scholarship, not research. The purpose of this project, however, is to demonstrate that Practitioner Inquiry can attend to the rigors of empirical research. The next section traces the move toward empirical research in the writing center studies and details its expectations and criteria, situating the kairos for this project.

Empirical Research: Answering the Call

In "NCTE/CCCC's Recent War on Scholarship" (2005), an article that would prove to have far-reaching impact in the field of Composition Studies, Richard Haswell brought attention to the general lack of what he termed RAD research represented in scholarship on teaching composition at the postsecondary level. Haswell roundly critiques our "flagstaff houses," the National Council of the Teachers of English (NCTE) and Conference on College Composition and Communication (CCCC), saying that while they claim to support a broad range of scholarship, they have systematically denied sponsorship of "empirical inquiry, laboratory studies, data gathering, experimental investigation..." (p. 200). These kinds of research Haswell categorizes as RAD research, which he defines as

> a best effort inquiry into the actualities of a situation, inquiry that is explicitly enough systematized in sampling, execution, and analysis to be replicated; exactly enough circumscribed to be extended; and factually enough supported to be verified.
>
> (p. 201)

Haswell makes the case that as a mode of research valued by almost every other discipline, RAD research hardly needs defending, asserting that systematized, data-based inquiry has implications for the sustainability of a discipline.

Although Haswell's critique was directed at composition studies in general, the article has maintained a notable presence in writing studies scholarship. Indeed, many of the scholars I will discuss in the ensuing literature review mention this 2005 article as one impetus for their inquiry. Yet, while Haswell's critique resonated across writing center studies, his project, in many ways, culminates discussions of research practices circling in the field for over 15 years. In 1984, looking back on the preceding decade of rapid growth of writing centers in the U.S. triggered by the open admissions initiatives of the 1970s, North (1984b) similarly takes issue with common practices loosely defined as research that falls short of the formal inquiry he sees as necessary to "test our assumptions" (p. 25). In particular, North asserts the need for writing center researchers "to create a methodology, one borrowed from disciplines like ethnography, social psychology, and cognitive psychology" (p. 29), to engage in research that is "complex and disruptive" (30), pointing to the need for disciplinary legitimation, and to prove that "writing centers work" (33).

While the concerns about research definitely altered and expanded in the ensuing years, the kind of assessment of research practices North undertakes has proven to be a sustained genre in the field. Fifteen years after North's essay, Gillespie et al.'s (2002) *Writing Center Research: Extending the Conversation* continued this exploration into the kinds of research being produced by writing center practitioners, noting "a need for more explicit talk about what we mean by research, what should count as research, and how to conduct research" (Gillam, 2002, p. xv). Like North, Gillespie et al. (2002) similarly identify the need for explication of methodology and critique of methods, noting it as an impetus for their book (p. xii). The sustainability of the field in 2002 does not seem quite as critical as it was for North in 1984; the significance of research for these authors, who apparently represented a broad sentiment of the field, lay in its implications for asserting agency over defining our work and its potential for disciplinary contributions.

Perhaps because of the political liminality of writing centers so often noted in the literature, and the perceived potential of research in efforts to establish institutional capital and afford practitioners agency over our own work, writing center practitioners have continued to produce assessments of current research practices, and, over time, with more explicit critiques and suggestions. As the article title suggests, Sarah Liggett, Kerri Jordan, & Steve Price's (2011) "Mapping Knowledge-Making in Writing Center Research: A Taxonomy of Methodologies" is not as interested in validating certain practices or demonstrating institutional value. Rather, the authors' concerns are more aligned with North (1984b) and Gillespie et al.'s (2002) call for explication of research methodologies to gauge the epistemological terrain of the field. Such assessments, however, eventually transformed into overt critiques. In "Theory, Lore, and More: An Analysis of RAD Research in *The Writing Center Journal*, 1980–2009," Dana Driscoll & Sherry Wynn Perdue's (2012) critical assessment of writing center publications culminates with a call to action. Specifically invoking Haswell (2005) and harkening to North's (1984b) need to "test our assumptions," they emphasize the need for RAD research in the writing center and advocate identifying frameworks and methods that support it in order to "validate our practices" (p. 29). To rate published writing center scholarship in terms of it being RAD research, Driscoll & Perdue designed a rubric with the following seven elements as areas for evaluation (pp. 20–21):

1   Background and Significance
2   Study Design and Data Collection
3   Selection of Participants and/or Texts
4   Method of Analysis
5   Presentation of Results
6   Discussion and Implications
7   Limitations and Future Work

The absence or limited articulation of many of these elements in a significant body of writing center research resulted in Driscoll & Perdue finding that only 5% of 270 articles published in *The Writing Center Journal* between 1980 and 2009 meet RAD criteria (p. 28).[6]

As scholars mobilized responses to Driscoll and Perdue's call, the focus shifted from Haswell's "RAD" research to the more widely employed "empirical research." With his articulation that "RAD scholarship may be feminist, empirical, ethnomethodological, contextual, action, liberatory, or critical" (202), Haswell makes clear that his notion of RAD research includes, but is not exclusively tied to, empirical research. While it is also important to note that this list suggests false distinctions as none of these approaches are necessarily mutually exclusive when designing a research project, empirical research has indisputably received the most attention from writing center practitioners responding to calls for RAD research. In *Researching the Writing Center: Towards an Evidence-Based Practice*, Rebecca Day Babcock & Terese Thonus (2012), for example, foreground calls for RAD research as an impetus for their project that argues for empirical inquiry, suggesting that such inquiry is an obvious culmination to the kinds of research long privileged among writing center practitioners: "While theoretical investigations build the foundation for writing center studies, and anecdotal experience points in the direction of best practices, empirical research will create a credible link between the two" (p. 3). Similarly focused on producing empirical research in writing center contexts, Jackie Grutsch McKinney's (2015) *Strategies for Writing Center Research* provides a detailed account of strategies for conducting empirical research from research proposal through the presentation of data. Analogous to McKinney's work in its focus on supporting empirical research, but targeted specifically to novice undergraduate researchers, Joyce Kinkead's (2016) *Researching Writing: An Introduction to Research Methods* walks a reader through setting up and designing a study with discussion of a range of approaches. Jo Mackiewicz and Rebecca Babcock (2020) continue these efforts to provide resources and references to support empirical research with their collection, *Theories and Methods of Writing Center Studies: A Practical Guide*. Most notable about this volume in terms of the discussion here, in addition to the examples of methods that have been applied in writing center studies (which make up the second of two sections), is the inclusion of a section devoted to different theories to guide research (the first section.) The authors of the individual chapters take up questions such as why a theory or method is employed, examples of that application, and research questions that a theory or method is particularly well suited to address. (p. 1).

Three titles in particular have taken these efforts to the next step by providing full-length treatments of single study: *The Aboutness of Writing Center Talk: A Corpus-Driven and Discourse Analysis* (Mackiewicz, 2017), *Talk about Writing: The Tutoring Strategies of Experienced Writing Center Tutors* (Mackiewicz & Thompson, 2018), and

Writing Center Talk over Time: A Mixed-Method Study (Mackiewicz, 2018). Each of these monographs provides readers with a detailed research design explaining the approaches and methods used in the described study.[7] These contributions are significant in that they move us to having comprehensive examples of single studies from beginning to end with detailed description of methods used in application of specific analytical frameworks. However, I would argue they do not include a methodology as I am using the term here—a guiding construct that informs the practitioner's stance—the ethics and considerations that guide their approach to the research design and how they interact with their research participants/students (and even the larger research context). I am not suggesting such concerns were not considered by the researchers mentioned, but simply that a methodology guiding such concerns was not described in their research design.

The timing and focus of these projects point to the kairos for engaging empirical research practices in the field right now. And if we are to continue to move this empirical inquiry project forward, clearly we need models specifically designed to address the concerns and values of writing center practitioners. Following the trajectory of scholarship, from assessments (North, 1984; Gillespie et al., 2002; Liggett, Jordan, & Price, 2011), critiques and calls (Haswell, 2005; Driscoll & Perdue, 2012), to responses that feature samplings of research designs from comparable disciplines (Babcock & Thonus, 2012), guides to theories, methods, and strategies for conducting empirical research (Grutsch McKinney, 2015; Mackiewicz & Babcock, 2020), and finally to examples of research designs applied in full-length studies (Mackiewicz, 2017, 2018; Mackiewicz & Thompson, 2018), the logical culminating contribution to these efforts is the explication of a complete research model that encompasses a methodology articulated with methods alongside examples of application to demonstrate efficacy. To have real currency with researchers in the field, such a model would need to be readily accessible, incorporate characteristics and practices commonly engaged and valued, yet offer enough flexibility to be tailored to individual contexts and agendas. Thus, a good place to begin is with a methodology already in use.

Practitioner Inquiry as a Viable Response

With the exception of the three full-length studies, all the works discussed in the previous section include mention, in one way or another,[8] of Practitioner Inquiry/research as commonly employed in writing center research, making it an obvious choice to explore potentiality;

however, the context surrounding those mentions must be heeded as well. For example, while consistently treated in taxonomies and assessments of research, little, if any, published writing center scholarship or research specifically notes Practitioner Inquiry (or practitioner research) as its research design. Despite its prominence in discussions of research taxonomies—and obvious application in various forms in writing center research—searches of the terms "Practitioner Inquiry"/"practitioner research"/"teacher research" combined with "writing center" in several online databases, including CompPile, ERIC, and MLA, turn up at most 35 results. When Practitioner Inquiry is acknowledged, it is often relegated as "informal" research (Babcock & Thonus, 2012, p. 18). Grutsch McKinney (2015), having highlighted scholarship as distinct from research (p. xvii) in her monograph, defines Practitioner Inquiry as "*scholarship* [emphasis added] in which an author uses his or her own experience as evidence" (p. 158). In general, while these mentions suggest it has some value amongst writing center scholars, many caution Practitioner Inquiry can easily fall into the trap of being little more than "lore" (Gillespie, 2002), or, as Mackiewicz & Babcock (2020) suggest, having value (especially when employed with rigor) but limited to providing "springboards" for further investigation (p. 7).

However, it is these perceptions of Practitioner Inquiry that are limiting, particularly in that they do not reflect how Practitioner Inquiry is treated as a rigorous mode of research in other fields, particularly education.[9] A database search similar to the one mentioned earlier, but excluding "writing center," yields a far more robust body of scholarship—especially from Google Scholar, which returns results numbering in the thousands, even with the date restricted to entries later than 2016. Further complicating these recent categorizations of Practitioner Inquiry by writing center scholars are earlier treatments in the field that identify a range in how Practitioner Inquiry is employed, frequently using the terms *formal* and *informal* as categories. Gillam (2002), for example, explicitly notes that empirical work "refer[s] to a broad category of research that includes case studies, ethnography, and various forms of practitioner inquiry" (p. xvi), and goes on to note that forms of Practitioner Inquiry that "couple qualitative empirical research...with theoretical speculation" are valued over others (p. xxii). Unfortunately, the more recent representations of Practitioner Inquiry as a relatively informal mode of inquiry have resulted in its potential to guide empirical research remaining unrealized.

Notwithstanding that the prevalent "this-is-what-we-do-at-our-center" construct is often associated with Practitioner Inquiry, in and of itself, this approach does not constitute Practitioner Inquiry. Practitioner Inquiry does provide space for telling our stories, but it also demands practices aligned with empirical research. Too often, however, thorough explication of processes, practices, and data is left out in published writing center research categorized as Practitioner Inquiry. Yet, taxonomical work still points to its prevalence. As noted earlier, Gillam (2002) categorizes Practitioner Inquiry as empirical research as opposed to conceptual, and almost ten years later, Liggett, Jordan, & Price (2011), perhaps responding to the inconsistencies surrounding formal/informal descriptors, identify Practitioner Inquiry as one of three main research approaches in their taxonomy, distinct from both empirical and conceptual. This attention to Practitioner Inquiry in meta-analyses of our research suggests that we are employing it as a research framework, albeit to varying extents in terms of demonstrating rigor and data integrity. This raises the question: if Practitioner Inquiry is noted as common in surveys of research designs, why is it not specifically named in the research itself? I suggest one reason for this lack is the absence of a formalized articulation of Practitioner Inquiry as a research model in our field. Defining Practitioner Inquiry in such a way will entail illustrating how concepts necessary for rigorous empirical research, like systematicity, triangulation, and transferability, not only align with its theoretical goals but can be enacted as part of current common practices.

These treatments of Practitioner Inquiry also suggest an overall reluctance to dismiss it as ineffective despite its shortcomings; after all, such scholarship does inform many of our practices in important ways. Moreover, looking at its application in contexts outside of writing centers, particularly in education, points to its appropriateness in that it is being used to explore issues aligned with the concerns of writing center practitioners. Recent studies that focus on identifying best practices to promote acquisition of science terminology by language+ learners (Williams, Pringle, & Kilgore, 2019), promoting teacher professional development through research (Cheng & Li, 2020; Kondo, 2020), assessing the efficacy of classroom pedagogy and approaches using Universal Design Learning (Boothe, Lohmann, & Owiny, 2020), or themed writing workshops (Kinberg, 2020) are but a small sampling of the many studies employing Practitioner Inquiry into topics that parallel similar interest and concerns in writing center studies. I am suggesting, therefore, that if we are to heed Driscoll & Perdue's (2012) recommendation for "serious shifts in how writing center scholars conceptualize, conduct, compose and support research" (p. 29), we need to, like Babcock and Thonus suggest, articulate research models that accommodate working with data sources consistent with those commonly used in our field, namely qualitative data. But we also need to move beyond getting excited about isolated data sources, like surveys or inferred outcomes from participant observation. While isolated data events can become the impetus for a more robust study, to count as research, a researcher must also identify methodologies and methods, including triangulation (which requires multiple data sources), to ensure the research model is designed to support the values and goals of writing center practitioners and demonstrate veracity and validity. A clearly defined Practitioner Inquiry research model will not only allow us to engage in the kinds of research we find suitable to our contexts, but also provide a systematic approach for demonstrating the efficacy of common writing center practices with experiential evidence, which can help codify our research trajectories and further legitimize our work in broader academic discussions.

While these objectives are formidable in and of themselves, a viable model must also provide for ways to enact the theoretical concepts that guide our practice, such as access, inclusivity, and collaboration. In Chapter 1, I begin by emphasizing my understanding that certain theoretical constructs, specifically collaboration, underpin all our work. This chapter is born out of my concern over invocations of collaboration that leave practices uninterrogated and rely on the inherent claims of "collaboration" to demonstrate efficacy. To explore the possibilities of fully realizing collaboration in our research and practice, which necessarily include transparent and robust explications, I look to sources not commonly engaged in our field for models, specifically the work of Indigenous Pacific scholars. As these scholars have codified collaboration in ways that support sustainability and communal well-being within complex societal structures, I argue that Indigenous theories can teach us a lot about collaboration—working together, supporting inclusion and linguistic diversity, and, at the same time, mediating hegemonic structures in our contemporary contexts. I provide a heuristic of processes for enacting collaboration that adapts these theories for both practice and research so as to attend to the concerns, knowledge, and values of all participants and stakeholders in our complex contemporary contexts.

The work of Chapter 2 is to describe Practitioner Inquiry as a model. I begin by defining Practitioner Inquiry with a methodology that foregrounds concepts foundational in writing center work, such as collaboration. This project diverts from other similar projects in that I then articulate methods and practices designed to facilitate the theoretical goals of the methodology; for example, how collaboration with research participants can be enacted from the inception of a research project through completion. I map existing models of Practitioner Inquiry, highlighting commonalities and limitations, examining where we might benefit from adopting or adapting certain approaches and processes. I then explicate a model of Practitioner Inquiry that merges these models and incorporates elements from other qualitative research methodologies, specifically the concepts of triangulation, systematicity, and transferability, so that application of Practitioner Inquiry is more likely to produce empirical research appropriate for writing center and other similar educational contexts.

Chapter 3 is the first of two designed to demonstrate applications of Practitioner Inquiry. It presents a pilot study in which Practitioner Inquiry was implemented to guide both practice and research in our center to examine the intersections between collaboration at the administrative level and consultant professionalization. I explain how we enacted collaboration as part of a Practitioner Inquiry methodology in the administration of our center, specifically focusing on the interactions between consultants and the director. At the same time, Practitioner Inquiry guides the mixed-methods study into the implications of collaboration on consultant professionalization. Findings from both qualitative excerpts and in vivo coding of end-of-semester consultant evaluations were used to investigate four concepts correlated with acquiring professionalization: Agency, Support, Investment, and Learning, to which I add a fifth, Collaboration. This study contributes to recent scholarship (Kail, Gillespie, & Hughes, 2019) on the benefits of writing center work for consultants through an empirical investigation into consultant professionalization *vis-à-vis* collaboration in the less-examined subtopic of the director-consultant relationship, and illustrates the efficacy of Practitioner Inquiry as a methodology to guide both practice and research.

In Chapter 4, I present a study conducted at both the University of Hawai'i at Mānoa, my home campus, and the National University of Ireland at Galway, where I worked in their writing center for a semester, to investigate a concern often expressed by consultants about the disconnect between supporting translingual literacy practices as a writer's agency and teaching/promoting academic discourse. While Chapter 3 describes application of Practitioner Inquiry to guide collaborative practices in day-to-day administrative interactions and then assesses them, this chapter details a collaborative construct to working with consultants as participants in Practitioner Inquiry research. As will be discussed in Chapter 1, Indigenous approaches to collaboration emphasize the importance of formulating a study in response to the concerns of research participants. In this project, I collaborate with consultants through interviews to draw from their expertise in an investigation into this consultant-driven question. In applying the same study at two sites, the chapter demonstrates the transferability of Practitioner Inquiry and provides opportunity to compare data gathered from consultants at different locations in terms of congruency on the issue of supporting translingual literacy practices.

Summary

I began this chapter explaining how where I live and practice has greatly influenced my investment in empirical research. The abuses that have been committed in the name of research, too many of which have resulted in the misrepresentation and subsequent marginalization of peoples and their cultures, highlight the importance of accounting for multiple variables and constantly interrogating the analytical lens through which experiences and data are viewed. I would be remiss if I did not acknowledge that many such studies, particularly those that occurred within Native communities, did employ methods aligned with empirical research. This history has only sedimented my commitment to articulating methodologies to guide methods and practices employed in research to ensure research is ethical and serves not only my own purposes and interests but those of the research participants I work with. In my own work as a center director, I am committed to transparency and providing opportunities so that the students I work with, whether consultants or visitors to the center, have an easier time negotiating issues of access whether that be in academia or the private sector. I want to honor the knowledge and expertise they bring and collaborate with them in ways that disrupt hierarchical structures, both within the academy and in their wider communities, in the service of their interests. I firmly believe ethical empirical research is one way to realize these goals, and to ensure our work is ethical, we need to foreground theories that emphasize our values and priorities. My hope is that the model I explicate in the ensuing chapters not only makes evident these objectives but is presented in such a way that researchers, whether new to the game or experienced hands, can easily see ways this model can work in and for their contexts.

Notes

1 In our center, we use "consultants" rather than tutors, and I will do the same throughout.
2 This is not to imply that research should proceed in some static and predefined order. For example, recursive practices, which will be more fully

discussed in Chapter 2, are an essential element of the Practitioner Inquiry model I present, indicating that certain parts of the research process can and should be revisited and reconsidered as often as is necessary to ensure accuracy.
3 Cochran-Smith & Lytle (2009) also point to the rigor tied to Practitioner Inquiry, noting Validity, Generalizability, and Systematicity all as key features (pp. 43–44); I will revisit these elements to explain how they are adapted for the model I present in Chapter 2.
4 Linguistic scholars use stance to explain the response one interlocutor has when interacting with others in sociocultural contexts. Its application in Linguistics differs from how I am adapting it here, but the overarching premises are transferable.
5 There are variations in the scholarship of the terms I focus on here (i.e., assessments and appraisal for evaluation), but I find the differences not significant enough for the purposes of my application.
6 Driscoll & Perdue determined 90 articles out of 270 published in *WCJ* during that time period could be considered research; of that 90, 16% could be categorized as RAD research, while 16% reflects approximately 5% of the total 270 articles.
7 The three volumes cover the following approaches for working with data: corpus-driven and conversation discourse analysis (*The Aboutness of Writing Center Talk*), mixed-methods using corpus-driven and qualitative analysis (*Writing Center Talk over Time*), and a theory-based coding scheme (*Talk about Writing*).
8 Stephen North refers to practitioners in a section called "Reflections on Experience" (p. 25), which would arguably align with other representations of Practitioner Inquiry.
9 These perceptions could also be remnants of attitudes reproduced by the hegemonic structures that resulted in teachers traditionally being marginalized in comparison to researchers in academia—structures that have also resulted in the marginalization of writing centers.

References

Babcock, R. D., & Thonus, T. (2012). *Researching the writing center: Towards an evidence-based practice.* New York, NY: Peter Lang Publishing Inc.

Boothe, K. A., Lohmann, M. J., & Owiny, R. (2020). Enhancing student learning in the online instructional environment through the use of universal design for learning. *Networks: An Online Journal for Teacher Research, 22*(1), 1–26.

Cheng, M. M. H. & Li, D. D. Y. (2020). Implementing practitioner research as a teacher professional development strategy in an Asia-Pacific context. *Journal of Education for Teaching: Internation.al Research and Pedagogy, 46*(1), 55–70.

Cochran-Smith, M., & Lytle, S. (1999a). Relationships of knowledge and practice: Teacher learning in communities. *Review of Research in Education, 24*, 249–305.

Cochran-Smith, M., & Lytle, S. (1999b). The teacher research movement: A decade later. *Educational Researcher, 28*(7), 15–25.

Cochran-Smith, M., & Lytle, S. (2009). *Inquiry as stance: Practitioner research for the next generation.* New York, NY: Teachers College Press.

Denny, H. C. (2010). *Facing the center: Toward an identity politics of one-to-one mentoring.* Logan: Utah State University Press.

Dictionary.com. (n.d.). Practitioner. In *Dictionary.com.* Retrieved June 2, 2020, from https://www.dictionary.com/browse/practitioner

Driscoll, D. L., & Perdue, S. W. (2012). Theory, lore, and more: An analysis of RAD research in *The Writing Center Journal,* 1980–2009. *The Writing Center Journal, 3*(22), 11–39.

Du Bois, J. W. (2007). The stance triangle. In R. Englebretson (Ed.), *Stancetaking in discourse: Subjectivity, evaluation, interaction* (pp. 139–182). Amsterdam: John Benjamins Publishing.

Gillam, A. (2002). Introduction. In P. Gillespie, A. Gillam, L. F. Brown, & B. Stay (Eds.), *Writing center research: Extending the conversation* (pp. 39–51). Mahwah, NJ: Lawrence Erlbaum Associates.

Gillespie, P. (2002). Beyond the house of lore: Writing center as research site. In P. Gillespie, A. Gillam, L. F. Brown, & B. Stay (Eds.), *Writing center research: Extending the conversation* (pp. 39–51). Mahwah, NJ: Lawrence Erlbaum Associates.

Gillespie, P., Gillam, A., Brown, L. F., & Stay, B. (Eds.). (2002). *Writing center research: Extending the conversation.* Mahwah, NJ: Lawrence Erlbaum Associates.

Goswami, D., & Stillman, P. (1987). *Reclaiming the classroom: Teacher research as an agency for change* (p. 242). Upper Montclair, NJ: Boynton/Cook Publishers, Inc.

Grutsch McKinney, J. (2015). *Strategies for writing center research.* Anderson, SC: Parlor Press.

Harding, S. (1987). Introduction: Is there a feminist method? In S. Harding (Ed.), *Feminism and methodology: Social science issues* (pp. 1–14). Bloomington: Indiana University Press.

Haswell, R. H. (2005). NCTE/CCCC's recent war on scholarship. *Written Communication, 22*(2), 198–223.

Joseph, C. (2018). 10 Characteristics of professionalism. *Small Business-Chron. com.* Retrieved from http://smallbusiness.chron.com/10-characteristics-professionalism-708.html.

Kail, H, Gillespie, P., & Hughes, B. (2019). *The peer writing tutor alumni research project.* Retrieved from http://www.writing.wisc.edu/pwtarp/

Kinberg, M. (2020). Real-life nature-based experiences as keys to the writing workshop. *Networks: An Online Journal for Teacher Research, 22*(1). Retrieved from https://doi.org/10.4148/2470-6353.1308.

Kinkead, J. (2016). *Researching writing: An introduction to research methods.* Logan: Utah State University Press.

Kondo, T. (2020). Transforming critical and participative teacher research into communicative action: A possible direction for teacher professional learning. *Educational Action Research, 28*(2), 159–174.

Liggett, S., Jordan, K., & Price, S. (2011). Mapping knowledge-making in writing center research: A taxonomy of methodologies. *Writing Center Journal, 31*(2), 50–88.

Mackiewicz, J. (2017). *The aboutness of writing center talk: A corpus-driven and discourse analysis.* New York, NY: Routledge.

Mackiewicz, J. (2018). *Writing center talk over time: A mixed-method study.* New York, NY: Routledge.

Mackiewicz, J., & Babcock, R. (2020). *Theories and methods of writing center studies: A practical guide.* New York, NY: Routledge.

Mackiewicz, J., & Thompson, I. (2018). *Talk about writing: The tutoring strategies of experienced writing center Tutors* (Vol. 1). New York, NY: Routledge.

Merriam-Webster. (n.d.). Practitioner. In *Merriam-Webster.com dictionary.* Retrieved from https://www.merriam-webster.com/dictionary/practitioner

Mindtools Content Team. (2019). Professionalism: Developing this vital characteristic. *Mindtools, Essential Skills for an Excellent Career.* Retrieved from https://www.mindtools.com/pages/article/professionalism.htm.

Nordstrom, G. (2003). Finding their way to the writing center: Language perceptions of Pidgin speakers and non-native speakers from Asian countries. *The Writing Lab Newsletter, 28*(3), 8–11.

Nordstrom, G., Furtado, N., Gushiken, G., Ito-Fujita, A., Iwashita, K., Kurashige, N., Togafau, K., & Wang, I. (Fall 2019). Affirming our liminality & writing on the walls: How we welcome in our writing center." *The Peer Review Journal, 3*(1). Retrieved from http://thepeerreview-iwca.org/issues/redefining-welcome/affirming-our-liminality-writing-on-the-walls-how-we-welcome-in-our-writing-center/

North, S. M. (1984a). The idea of a writing center. *College English, 46*(5), 433–446.

North, S. M. (1984b). Writing center research: Testing our assumptions. In G. A. Olson (Ed.), *Writing centers: Theory and administration* (pp. 24–35). Urbana, IL: NCTE.

Ray, R. (1993). *The practice of theory. Teacher research in composition.* Urbana, IL: NCTE.

Stenhouse, L. (1983). *Authority, education, and emancipation: A collection of papers.* Portsmouth, NH: Heinemann Educational Books.

Williams, R., Pringle, R., & Kilgore, K. (2019). A Practitioner's inquiry into vocabulary building strategies for native Spanish speaking ELLs in inquiry-based science. *Research in Science Education, 49*(4), 989–1000.

1 What Indigenous Practices Can Teach Us about Collaboration

Since my first forays into empirical research as a master's student, I have been consumed with the ethics and implications of all aspects of my work. I know this is a result of where I grew up and the impact research and educational policies have had in Hawaiʻi, the islands I call home. Like many other locations in the Pacific and across the United States, there is a history of using the educational system to disenfranchise the Native people and other marginalized groups, particularly through the banning of the Indigenous language as a medium of education and academic/government-sanctioned research programs that exploit non-white peoples and their lands. As the title suggests, in this chapter, I will draw from Indigenous concepts and approaches to articulate a theory of collaboration for practitioners[1] in their research, teaching, and service. I therefore want to begin with an Indigenous voice to capture how this legacy is experienced by those being "researched," "taught," and "helped." The poem, "Natives Wanted," by Kanaka Maoli (Native Hawaiian[2]) poet and scholar Brandy Nālani McDougall (2010) satirizes the self-serving, abusive exploitation and violence too many Euro-Western settlers/researchers have visited on Indigenous peoples as they moved through the Pacific and other colonized locations. It represents tragic and enduring scenarios all too familiar in McDougall's home islands, and is illustrative of the irresponsible and unethical practices that have worked to serve settler colonialism—practices my own practitioner stance responds to:

Natives Wanted

Do you still hunt and/or gather?
Continue to use plants for healing?
Do you have a dying language
or live in a remote corner

of an island or rainforest?
Have you contracted foreign diseases
And are now facing cultural extinction?
Do you consistently reject the teachings
of missionaries and settlers?
Do you still chant, sing, and/or dance
as your ancestors did? Do you continue
to revere and/or worship your ancestors?
Do you still wear traditional attire
(i.e., loincloths, feathers, animal skins
or fur, bark cloth, leaves, etc.)
and/or pierce and/or tattoo and/or scar
any part of your body? Have you
maintained your oral traditions
and thus, received sacred knowledge
passed down for at least 5 generations?
Do you now or have you ever
practiced human sacrifice and/or eaten
your enemies (or your friends/family)?
Do you have a long history of burying
priceless treasures with your dead
and still know where they are buried?

If you can answer "yes" to 3 or more of the above
question, then you are an ideal subject of study
for anthropologists, archaeologists, pharmaceutical
companies, natural historians, museum curators,
colonial writers, missionaries and tourists.

Disclaimer: Compensation for all sacred artifacts and knowledge
may be promised though generally not guaranteed. Side effects
of study may include (but are not limited to): dispossession,
displacement, more disease, chronic colonization, exploitation,
diabetes, alcoholism/drug abuse, severe depression, paranoia,
spiritual crisis, and xenophobia.

(p. 51)

The thing about satire is there is always a truth to it. While someone not familiar with the context McDougall is writing within might foreground the satire so evident in the poem, I would caution against misreading it only as hyperbole. Too much of what is detailed in the poem has been the reality of Indigenous peoples since representatives of the West stumbled onto the lands of their flourishing nations. Complex social and governmental systems were often dismissed as primitive, and the unfamiliar cultures deemed inferior, but nevertheless prime for research. This research, while designed to acquire "knowledge" for the researcher, too frequently worked to reinforce colonial claims to Indigenous land, property (intellectual and cultural), and bodies, without consideration of the impact of that research on individuals or their communities.

The concept of *research* in Western contexts is almost always a grand narrative in and of itself. Without a voice from the Other(s') side to convey what it is like to be a victim of it, research is most often understood in the West as corresponding to intellectual engagement, innovation, and progress. Although McDougall's poem obviously focuses on research, the exploitation, oppression, and disenfranchisement she refers to have been analogous across social contexts, including governmental, judicial, and educational institutions. The history and outcomes of Western contact are real and present as I write this chapter, and they inform who I am as a member of this community and my work as a practitioner. I suspect that some may counter by arguing that such extreme conditions no longer occur, or that what happens in our classrooms and centers does not align with such violence. I, however, work with many Indigenous students as well as students from other marginalized groups who can recount experiences when their language practices, ethnicity, or other cultural identifiers have resulted in their being marked as inferior, denied access, or otherwise disenfranchised in the academy. Their experiences are manifestations of the "Disclaimer" detailed in McDougall's poem that points not only to the consequences for those directly impacted by these scientific undertakings but also to the ongoing intergenerational trauma it causes. A March 3, 2020, *Star Advertiser* (Hawai'i's main newspaper) article, "After over a Century in England, 20 Native Hawaiian Skulls Return Home to Hawaii" [sic], is but one more example of how the trauma of being objectified for science to satisfy colonial curiosity continues to be leveraged. The article begins by explaining an all too familiar scenario: "Human remains taken from Hawaii in the name of science have been returned to the islands after more than a century in a museum in England" (Hurley, 2020). It is this sociohistorical context that this chapter responds to, as I believe enacting a critical collaborative practice can engender awareness of and provide strategies to counter hegemonic and oppressive constructs both in and out of the academy.

In general, the premise that collaboration counters institutionalized hegemonies is not new. Indeed, early efforts to theorize collaboration increasingly foregrounded subverting hierarchical structures in the academy. Responding to the "social turn" in writing studies that began in the 1980s, scholars such as Kenneth Bruffee (1984), John Trimbur (1989), and Andrea Lunsford & Lisa Ede (1992) shaped robust conversations focused on understanding the intellectual and ethical potential of collaboration. It is much more challenging, however, to find comparable works authored over the last two decades. Not only does it seem that treatments of collaboration have lost the rigor of these earlier discussions, this absence of theoretical grounding or interrogation of techniques for practice has left us ill-equipped to deal with the changing dynamics of our classrooms and in our research. For writing center practitioners specifically, while we have become more and more informed about the inherent hierarchical contingencies in our spheres of practice, our efforts to identify best practices to meet the demands of this work have not included rethinking how we understand and perform collaboration, its potential, and limitations. Thus, while collaboration has remained a prominent theme in our work, interrogation of what exactly makes an act collaborative, or the degree to which collaboration is attained, has waned. We use the word all the time, and I suspect in most cases we are enacting it in some form, but just what that form is, how it attends to the goals of a collaborative practice, and how those goals change across contexts remain largely under-discussed.

Since first contemplating writing this chapter, I have often thought of a passage by Mary Louise Pratt (2008) on reciprocity: "Reciprocity has always been capitalism's ideology of itself….[reciprocity] is one of the stories it tells itself about itself. The difference between equal and unequal exchange is suppressed" (p. 84). The element of Pratt's argument that resonates with my purposes here is the propensity by any group to claim a positive attribute such as reciprocity without interrogating the extent to which actions designed to enact reciprocity are truly reciprocal for those on the other side of the interaction. I have become increasingly concerned that the same argument can be applied to collaboration. To say that "collaboration" is common in our work is an understatement; it is often featured in book and article titles, and in conference themes and presentations. In writing center studies, collaboration is the concept at the very foundation of our practice. While I do not think that these widespread applications are problematic *per se*, the lack of explanation about what is meant by the word when it is invoked could be. The importance of collaboration to so much of our work demands that we constantly revisit how we engage with such a significant concept so we can better understand how and the extent to which collaboration is achieved in any particular interaction. Simply put, there seems to be a propensity in the scholarship to simply make claims of collaboration rather than theoretically ground or explicate our instances of collaboration and the limitations of a collaborative act.

The basic goals of this chapter are to (1) articulate a theory of collaboration guided by ethical approaches and strategies that can be applied across our sites of practice, whether teaching, service, or research; and (2) promote an understanding that collaboration occurs on a continuum, and, as responsible scholars and practitioners, we should be cognizant of where our discrete acts of collaboration lie on that continuum. I will begin by mapping several dominant treatments of collaboration from writing studies scholars, noting how they represent evolving efforts to acknowledge, then question, and finally contest the hierarchical structures in our institutions. I then argue that to meet the demands of our increasingly diverse sites of practice, and to attend to the value we place on access, equity, and inclusivity, we can learn from Indigenous, specifically Kanaka Maoli, approaches and practices. I look to these approaches and practices as they embody lifeways that support holistic manifestations of collaboration that extend beyond discreet interactions or a focus only on individuals. They can work to remind practitioners of the importance of understanding our interactions as taking place in a larger web of concerns and interests that include the places we occupy. This expansive understanding of the reach of our actions can guide our practices to better attend to power dynamics as well as varying concerns and experiences, and also highlights the need for us to acknowledge the impact of our work outside of academia. As histories of privileging and marginalization are increasingly laid bare in public discourse, to more fully attain our values of supporting diversity and inclusion, we need theories that complicate the normed assumptions about who our colleagues and students are and their lived realities, and push us to address the varied material conditions we all negotiate.

In many ways, the very concept of collaboration—co-laboring to attain an agreed-upon goal—does not naturally fit in the paradigm of traditional Western institutions and society. As many Euro-Western societies are built on the privileging of individualism, collaboration is arguably something better learned from communal societies.

For most Indigenous peoples, collaborative practices are integral in everyday interactions—their nations and communities are built on relationships defined by collaboration, with practices and ways of interacting less learned than intrinsic to one's state of being. Simply put, we can learn a lot from what Indigenous people have achieved over years of living in collaborative societies that work in conjunction with the environment as well as with each other. Their understandings of how such work should be performed and the expected results precede Western constructs designed to achieve similar outcomes. Moreover, as Indigenous scholars have had to respond to the abuses of Western research that serves ongoing settler colonialism, a significant body of Indigenous studies scholarship has articulated decolonial strategies that address institutionalized power structures and facilitate agency among research participants, and notably many of these practices foreground collaboration and reciprocity. I am not suggesting that all of our contacts in our academic contexts mirror the violence to which these treatments respond; however, such practices can provide a framework for dealing with inequities our students negotiate and mediate hierarchical structures reproduced within the academy.

The great irony of this chapter is that I am writing it alone. I have spent many hours contemplating how to construct an ethos worthy of the discussion I intend to put forth about collaboration that balances the contradiction of my solitary authorship. Many scholars before me have challenged the notion of whether authors ever really write alone. After all, I am reading and responding to the scholarship on collaboration across interdisciplinary conversations as I write. I have also had many discussions about this chapter with colleagues and practitioners working in other disciplines and at different places across the Pacific, within the United States, and in Europe. I have thus tried to implement various practices in an effort to infuse this chapter with a collaborative voice. For example, I began this section by invoking a Kanaka Maoli poet and scholar, Brandy Nālani McDougall, and I will close it by recounting my request for permission to use her poem. When I asked if I could reprint "Natives Wanted," I also asked McDougall to suggest another of her poems that represents what a Kanaka Maoli would consider important research for their community, so I could illustrate the contrast. I had in my mind a poem that foregrounds Kanaka Maoli innovations and expertise, perhaps something about navigation or astronomy. I should not have been surprised, however, when she did not suggest another of her own poems. Rather, she suggested a poem by her kumu (teacher[3]), Kanaka Maoli activist, scholar, and poet Haunani Kay Trask (1999), one that points to the possibility of working together—a way for a haole (foreigner, but more commonly Caucasian/white) to be an ally, and the caution that necessarily precedes trust:

Love Between the Two of Us

I.
because I thought the *haole*
never admit wrong
without bitterness
and guilt
without attacking us
for uncovering them
I didn't believe you
I thought you were star-crossed
a Shakespearean figure
of ridiculous posturing
you know, to be or not to be
the missionary rescue team
about to save
a foul, "primitive" soul
with murder
in its flesh

II.
we all know *haole* "love"
bounded by race
and power and the heavy
fist of lust
(missionaries came
to save
by taking)
how could I possibly believe?
why should any Hawaiian believe?
but it is a year
and I am stunned
by your humility
your sorrow for my people
your chosen separation
from that which is *haole*
I wonder at the resolve
in your clear blue eye

III.
do you understand
the nature of this war?
(pp. 62–63)

McDougall's suggestion to include her kumu's poem instead of her own embodies a Kanaka Maoli epistemological tradition of moʻokūʻauhau (recognition of genealogy) which, in this instance, honors her intellectual heritage (Meyer, 2001). This idea that one's own knowledge builds upon that of those who come before you captures a sense of collaboration across generations not commonly found in Western contexts that valorize the individual and singular efforts. It also represents generosity, a way to honor one's intellectual genealogy and acknowledge a shared acclaim (see hoʻomanawanui, 2014, p. xxxii). The message in Trask's poem is equally profound as it suggests there are ways for those of us from non-Indigenous backgrounds to serve as allies to those who have been disenfranchised, to ensure there is space for people, whether they be students or research participants, to assert their voices in the face of power dynamics that do not privilege them. The poem also depicts the wariness Indigenous people rightly feel when approached by "well-meaning" foreigners, and the resilience in their ability to take a chance on a potential ally despite historic and ongoing injustices. Trask shares how one should demonstrate allyship—through humility, empathy, acknowledgement of past injustices, and an investment in speaking against them. It is a message of kuleana (right, privilege, concern, responsibility (Pukui & Elbert, 1986, p. 179)) and inclusivity, elements I hold are essential in a theory of collaboration.

Theorizing Collaboration in Writing Studies

While collaboration is often invoked in our scholarship, most mentions treat collaboration as a function of practice, with little or no explanation of what a collaborative act entailed or achieved. It is rather common for collaboration to be identified as a keyword or in the title of a project; indeed, since Bruffee's landmark essay was published in 1984, a CompPile keyword search indicates 1,823 works that invoke collaboration (WAC, 2020). The question—or perhaps problem—resides in how collaboration is being invoked. There seems to be a propensity to note that some interaction was collaborative without any discussion as to how or why. It is not unusual for scholars to include phrases like, "this promoted a collaborative environment," "the project was collaborative," or "[insert group] worked collaboratively."[4] William Duffy (2014) captures this phenomenon, saying,

> collaboration has consequently assumed a catchall status that allows theorists and practitioners to deploy it in decidedly uncritical ways. To call something 'collaborative' is tantamount to saying nothing particular at all, except perhaps that two or more people have worked together in some capacity.
>
> (p. 417)

And as for defining collaboration, Duffy (2014) chastises against the tendency to "rely on definition by example because we have grown accustomed to invoking collaboration as a floating signifier without a specific referent" (p. 420). The penchant to simply name something collaborative without qualifying the claim correlates to a general lack of interrogation as to how an interaction is collaborative, and the degree to which collaboration is experienced across all participants.

I want to stress here, I am not arguing for a utopian parity, but rather an awareness that just saying an engagement is collaborative does not really tell us very much at all. The superficial nature of many treatments suggests a need for a deeper understanding of not only what counts as collaboration but also of what we can and should expect from collaborative practice and events. Perhaps the best place to start this work is with the meaning of the word. According to *The Online Etymology Dictionary* (Etymonline, 2020), collaboration is a relatively new word, incorporated into use around 1830, and simply means "the act of working together, united labor." Merriam-Webster's (2020) definition states "to work jointly with others or together especially in an intellectual endeavor."[5] While not explicit in these definitions, generally speaking, collaboration has come to imply a level of equality in an interaction, that everyone's opportunity to contribute is approximately the same and opinions are evenly recognized. How working together came to equate working equally in our understanding of collaboration is worthy of contemplation, especially considering that power structures inevitably inform most collaborative exchanges. Indeed, recognition of these uneven power dynamics is apparent in the dominant theories proposed by writing studies and writing center scholars, so examining how such structures are negotiated in articulations of respective theories provides some insights into evolving disciplinary perceptions of hierarchical and hegemonic systems and efforts to challenge them.

While, as Duffy (2014) notes, theoretical treatments of collaboration have waned in recent years, in the early decades of writing studies, several scholars articulated conceptual frameworks that have sustained. Tracing these dominant iterations of collaboration is instructive first and foremost because they capture how our disciplinary positions have changed in relation to society at large *vis-à-vis* how we view our roles in facilitating access and our understanding of the different ways silencing is experienced in the academy and other practice/research sites. In what follows, I provide an overview of several of the dominant theories on collaboration to lay the groundwork for the primary work of this chapter, which is to conceptualize collaboration so as to better address the social and political dynamics of our contemporary sites of practice.

Discussions of collaboration in the field invariably invoke Kenneth Bruffee's (1984) germinal article, "Collaborative Learning and the 'Conversation of Mankind.'" Bruffee notes peer tutoring, peer evaluation (what is also referred to as peer group workshopping), and group work in general as collaborative classroom practices that promote a kind of "indirect teaching in which the teacher sets the problem and organizes students to work it out collaboratively" (p. 637). In this model of collaborative learning, institutional power structures are unmasked, students become aware of them, but the endgame is still an ability to work, negotiate, and contribute to the "normal discourse" reproduced in and by the community to which one wishes to join, whether that be in government, business, or the academy. Bruffee would later be criticized for the perceived implication that collaboration ideally leads to the acquisition of "normal discourse" and assimilation into that discourse community. In this model, the growth of knowledge and critical recognition of hierarchical influences results from students' exposure to "abnormal" discourses, or discourses that include conventions not accepted in the identified discourse community, in this case the academy. This engagement with abnormal discourse engenders a meta awareness of normal discursive practices, but it unfortunately only leads to consensus about a new and improved normal discursive practice, leaving little room for alternative approaches or dissent in a collaborative exchange.

John Trimbur (1989) problematizes Bruffee's idea of abnormal discourse, importantly noting that abnormal discourse does not only appear at the convenience of an identified group of interlocutors; moreover, its impact does not always neatly result in an agreement on its influence. Rather, according to Trimbur, abnormal discourse "refers to dissensus, to marginalized voices, the resistance and contestation both within and outside the conversation" (p. 608). Ultimately, Trimbur argues, "To develop a critical version of collaborative learning, we will need to distinguish between consensus as an acculturative practice that reproduces business as usual and consensus as an oppositional one that challenges the prevailing conditions of production" (p. 612). Trimbur posits that collaboration does more than unmask hierarchical structures that reproduce dominant discursive practices in the academy and asserts that embracing dissensus has the power to "transform the reproductive apparatus" (p. 612). Trimbur's work moves from recognition of the power dynamics one is operating within in Bruffee's model to an awareness of the ways agency over discursive practices can work to resist and counter hegemonic forces in the academy and arguably the wider society.

Chronologically following Trimbur, Lunsford & Ede (1992) provide some of the most extensive work on theorizing collaboration in both writing and writing center studies. If Bruffee's model engenders awareness of power structures, and Trimbur's works to transform them, Lunsford and Ede point out that a "pure" collaborative interaction is an ideal, and that, in reality, collaboration occurs on a continuum. While much of Lunsford & Ede's work focuses specifically on writing collaboratively, unquestionably it is also applicable to the discussion here which includes writing center, classroom, and research practices. They offer theories of hierarchical and dialogic collaboration to account for the varied dynamics in collaborative interactions. Lunsford & Ede (1992) describe hierarchical collaboration as:

> Most common across disciplines and modes of production. It is carefully, and often rigidly, structured, driven by highly specific goals, and carried out by people playing clearly defined and delimited roles. These goals are most often designated by someone outside of and hierarchically superior to the immediate collaborative group or by a senior member or leader of a group. Because productivity and efficiency are of the essence in this mode of collaboration, the reality of multiple voices and shifting authority are seen as difficulties to be overcome or resolved.
>
> (p. 133)

Unlike previous projects that only (or mostly) consider collaboration between peers (i.e., faculty-to-faculty; student-to-student), hierarchical collaboration accounts for interactions that frequently occur in real-word settings where, despite participants having unequal power, collaboration does occur in various ways.

Lunsford & Ede (1992) thus provide a model for collaboration that captures the way working together and united labor does not automatically correlate to a level playing field among participants. I am thinking here of the kinds of small group work noted by Bruffee and Trimbur that so many of us often employ in our courses. Members of these small groups might be equal in that they are all students, but often the teacher somehow decides how the groups are formed and dictates to varying degrees what they will discuss. When we describe such group work as collaborative, we often ignore the obvious and disproportionate agency of the teacher. I am not suggesting that it would always be ideal or even practical for students to organize themselves and identify what they want to discuss (although I could see this working in some classes); however, uncritically identifying such scenarios as collaborative masks the teacher's role, and I suspect this can trickle down to a flattening of the inequity that may exist in intergroup dynamics. Within a group, for example, there is also often hierarchical positioning with someone appointing themselves a convener or facilitator, and perhaps others who step back while one or two members take charge. The hierarchical model promotes an understanding that individuals can collaborate despite varying levels of agency over the interaction and reminds us to be aware of and attend to that inequality.

Lunsford & Ede (1992) identify another form of collaboration, though not as common as hierarchical, and they coin it dialogic collaboration, which they explain as:

> not as widespread in the professions we studied as the hierarchical mode, and in fact, its practitioners had difficulty describing it, finding language within which to inscribe their felt realities. This dialogic mode is loosely structured, and the roles enacted within it are fluid: one person may occupy multiple and shifting roles as a project progresses. In this mode, the process of articulating goals is often as important as the goals themselves and sometimes even more important. Furthermore, those participating in dialogic collaboration generally value the creative tension inherent in multivoiced and multivalent ventures. What those involved in hierarchical collaboration see as a problem to be solved, these individuals view as a strength to capitalize on and to emphasize. In dialogic collaboration, this group effort is seen as an essential part of the production—rather than the recovery—of knowledge and as a means of individual satisfaction within the group.
>
> (p. 133)

What I find so compelling about the dialogic mode is that it allows for an individual's strengths to vary over time as they move between roles, which suggests participants fluidly accommodate each other, indicating a supportive environment that engenders an acute awareness of each person's engagement and investment in the goal. While attractive, this kind of collaboration seems like it might take time to achieve as it implies a certain level of trust among participants. Lunsford & Ede caution against pitting these two models of collaboration as binary opposites. When taken together, I see them providing a framework for understanding collaboration as variable, manifesting in different ways under different circumstances, not necessarily in "good" or "bad" ways, but rather adapted to the rhetorical situation in which it is enacted and occurring along a continuum. By articulating these variations in collaborative acts, Lunsford & Ede draw attention to the importance of identifying what practices are being enacted as part of a collaboration and how doing so makes power dynamics within the interaction apparent. Their work reminds us that collaboration, in addition to not being static across situations, can also be fluid within a specific situation.

While there have been other treatments of collaboration, especially during this period from mid-1980s to early-1990s, Bruffee's, Trimbur's, and Lunsford & Ede's have had notable influence in the field. And although all these theorists invariably discuss collaboration primarily in terms of group writing, the concepts have been used productively to inform other classroom practices, in particular to decenter a teacher's authority, thus attending to two of the foci of this book, pedagogy and practice. In terms of research endeavors, the third prong of this project, scholars drawing on feminist theory further developed collaborative practices specifically for research. For example, Geza Kirsch & Joy Ritchie (1995), in their landmark essay "Beyond the Personal: Theorizing a Politics of Location in Composition Research," promote what were groundbreaking notions of how a researcher should interact with research participants: "we propose changes in research practices, such as collaborating with participants in the development of research questions, the interpretation of data at both the descriptive and interpretive levels, and the writing of research reports" (p. 8). The rhetorical move from the (at that time) commonly used term "research subjects" to "research participants" signals the changing dynamic Kirsch and Ritchie are advocating for. They then identify various stages of the research process at which a researcher would ideally collaborate with research participants. But Kirsch and Ritchie go a step further—they note that a researcher needs to interrogate their own positionality to make plain their agenda, motives, and biases to better account for their relative power in a research environment and how that positionality acts as a terministic screen when interpreting data:

> we propose that composition researchers theorize their locations by examining their experiences as reflections of ideology and culture, by reinterpreting their own experiences through the eyes of others...we assert the importance of interrogating the motives for our research and the unspoken power relationships with the 'subjects' of our research.
>
> (pp. 8–9)

Kirsch and Ritchie's ideas were novel to composition researchers and unquestionably changed ideas about what it meant to conduct ethical research. Interestingly though, their tenets for ethical research are often treated as exclusively appropriate for that context—they are not adapted to classroom practices for example, or to interactions among writing center administrators and staff. Too often, our well-intentioned agendas as classroom or center practitioners go uninterrogated in the way Kirsch and Ritchie advocate for researchers. So, while many of our pedagogical theories acknowledge the teacher's position of power, they often fall short of examining that positionality in terms of what gets taught and how student performances are assessed.

Because of my position as a practitioner, my teaching, service, and research are not mutually exclusive, something I assume I share with many who similarly identify. As explained in the Introduction to this volume, by definition, "practitioner" can be a teacher *or* someone working in an educational service context *or* some combination of the two, which writing center administrators will immediately recognize. This work is also not confined to the academy—practitioners work and research in community centers and a variety of educational sites for example. While work in writing and other kinds of centers is often traditionally categorized solely as a service, recent years have seen efforts to represent these contexts as pedagogical sites where teaching and learning happen multidirectionally; using writing centers as example, dynamic pedagogical exchanges occur between the administrator and consultants, between consultants, and then between a consultant and a writer. Thus, when looking to articulate a model of collaboration, it needs to be adaptable to teaching, service, and research.

Mirroring this research-teacher/service divide, in writing center studies, Practitioner Inquiry is generally invoked only to explain how it has been used in research (Liggett, Jordan, & Price, 2011).

In education, however, Practitioner Inquiry looks more like the model presented in this book. Marilyn Cochran-Smith & Susan Lytle (2009), two of the foremost scholars on teacher research, bring teaching, research, and practice together in their model of Practitioner Inquiry. As explained in the previous chapter, they moved from teacher-research to practitioner-research to more fully accommodate different teacher/service scenarios, the teaching that goes on in many service contexts, and vice versa. Correspondingly, while their ideas of collaboration, in many ways, align with those presented earlier, they are also articulated to be adaptable across roles and sites. For example, Cochran-Smith & Lytle (2009) connect collaboratively conducting research within sites of both teaching and service when they advocate "Researching and Writing with Teachers and Others," with the "Others" referring to other kinds of practitioners. And similar to Trimbur (1989) and Lunsford & Ede's (1992) models, they identify an integral aspect of this work as "exploring the tensions of collaboration," a clear indication that positioning within a collaborative interaction is not always equitable and often demands compromise and negotiation. They also note the importance of "collaboratively constructing knowledge" (p. 94), a statement used rather pervasively following the turn toward social constructionism, and that is meant to capture the give-and-take involved in meaning making. When Cochran-Smith & Lytle (2009) specifically mention collaboration, they give extensive examples of who they collaborate with (i.e., school-based practitioners, student teachers, supervisors, graduate students), and the tensions and complications inherent in these collaborations. They assert that the kinds of collaborative interactions with individuals representing different academic status (i.e., student-professor; writer-consultant) and across sites of practice have the power to "disrupt the culture of the university," but also caution that "the potential for silencing and the emergence of issues of power and control come with the territory of collaboration around practitioner research" (pp. 102–103). While Cochran-Smith & Lytle's model of Practitioner Inquiry encompasses the various sites of our work, in terms of collaboration specifically, what is missing in these treatments, too, is explication of what happens in these collaborations and what makes them collaborative.

The theories proposed by all the scholars mentioned here have been instrumental, as the evolutions of theories and practices can be mapped along an increasing awareness of socioeconomic, cultural, ethnic, and racial inequities as well as hierarchies depending upon institutional positions. But, as I began to more fully understand my own positionality and the ways the location I inhabit influences my work, I also recognized that I occupy a position of power even if I only account for the agency afforded me as a member of the academy. This prompted me to ask the following question: What does collaboration look like from a student's or research participant's perspective? Or from the perspective of individuals whose communities have been traditionally marginalized and disenfranchised? What I am proposing here is that we take the next step and move away from trying to conceptualize collaboration from the position of teacher/scholar/researcher—in other words, positions of relative power. Instead, to account for how to best act ethically when working with a community, why don't we ask members of such a community? Or, perhaps even better, would it not be worthwhile to see what we can learn from communities who have foregrounded collaboration in their societal structures for generations, peoples who understand too well because of their histories of disenfranchisement the ways some of our efforts of collaboration are inadequate. Perhaps, if we seek to learn from such a community who has a holistic understanding of collaborative efforts that is infused throughout their everyday practices, we can articulate a cohesive model of collaboration that can inform pedagogy, practice, and research.

Rethinking Collaboration through Indigenous Practices

In this section, I will be drawing from Indigenous approaches and practices to articulate a theory of collaboration; however, while "Indigenous" is often invoked as an identifier to highlight the commonalities of experiences and practices among Indigenous groups and nations, Indigenous peoples are not homogenous. I want to be careful here because, although I do think the concepts I discuss may have analogous renderings across many Indigenous nations, noting the specific community a scholar or concept is associated with is necessary so as to accurately contextualize it. Here, Kanaka Maoli approaches and practices are foregrounded as they are the Indigenous people of Hawai'i, and having lived most of my life in Hawai'i, these practices are ones I am most familiar with. It is important to note that many cultural approaches and practices are intended for specific cultural contexts. I am not suggesting a direct transference, nor that all of these concepts can or should work in our educational contexts exactly as they do in their intended original settings. Rather, I will discuss the ways certain Kanaka Maoli frameworks for interacting with the world can engender a more ethical and holistic model of collaboration within the distinct context of academia. I hope we can learn from Kanaka

Maoli concepts, approaches, and practices, not duplicate them. In this work, I am concerned with real and perceived cultural appropriation. So, to draw attention to the distinction between adopting and adapting, for example, while I discuss the concepts in what follows as they are engaged with by Kanaka Maoli scholars, when drawing from them to inform the tenets I propose, I explain the tenets and practices in English only so as to emphasize that how I attend to these concepts does not capture how they are realized by Kanaka Maoli, nor is it intended to. More substantially, I hope it is evident that at the very core of the values promoted by the concepts I discuss is a sense of responsibility to the entirety of an interaction—not just the people, but the place as well—the actual land. As the discussion that follows points to, incorporating aspects of these concepts into a theory of collaboration requires understanding ethical obligations as extending into our communities beyond the university. In Hawai'i, this means acknowledging issues surrounding sovereignty and land/water rights, as they are fundamental concerns in the Kanaka Maoli community, and supporting these interests is inherent to adapting the concepts.

As noted earlier in this chapter, collaboration only entered into common use around 1830 (Etymonline, 2020), which could explain why the word collaboration does not appear in the *Hawaiian Dictionary* (Pukui & Elbert, 1986), which was first published in 1957. I was actually very surprised by this, and so were several Kanaka Maoli scholars I spoke with, probably because of a general understanding that collaboration is integral to Kanaka Maoli ways of interacting with each other and their 'āina (lands). The inherency of collaboration is apparent when the words used to define collaboration (i.e., "the act of working together, united labor"; "to work jointly with others or together") are used as the search terms rather than the word "collaboration" itself. Searching the *Hawaiian Dictionary* (Pukui & Elbert, 1986) this way, the number of words that foreground akin behaviors are numerous. For example, following are a few of the words and phrases that share definitions that align with working together or working jointly:

- Laulima (cooperation, joint action; group of people working together),
- Lōkahi (unity, agreement, accord, unison, harmony),
- Alu like mai (work in unity! work together!),
- Hana like (hana: work, labor; like: alike, like, similar, resembling),
- Hana pū (hana: work, labor; pū: together, entirely, completely, also with)[6]

Similarly, ʻōlelo noʻeau (proverbs) provide insights into how collaboration is conceived in a Kanaka Maoli worldview. The ʻōlelo noʻeau, "E lauhoe mai na waʻa; i ke kā i ka hoe; i ka hoe, i ke kā; pae aku i ka ʻāina" ("Everybody paddle the canoes together; bail and paddle, paddle and bail, and the shore is reached/Pitch in with a will, everybody, and the work is quickly done") (Pukui, 1983, p. 40), uses paddling a canoe as an example of how collaboration is enacted, and at least two other ʻōlelo noʻeau that highlight collaboration in their message invoke canoe paddling. This relation is telling as those familiar with paddling[7] know that each member of the paddling team assumes a different role. The Lanikai Canoe Club (2020) explains, "Each seat in the canoe requires certain talents and needs from a paddler, and each seat comes with its own sets of challenges and responsibilities." While working together and even working in unity is essential in such an activity, each participant plays a unique role in accomplishing the end goal, indicating that concepts of equality and equity, either of which is often associated with collaboration in Western contexts, are not realized the same way in Indigenous constructions.

Some of the words I mention earlier I was familiar with, but how I learned the rest is also an example of how collaboration is, in many ways, part of the fabric of communal interactions for Kanaka Maoli. In our writing center, we have a conference/lounge area where people can work and quietly socialize. Named a Burkean Parlor by our consultants (Kurashige & Iwashita in Nordstrom et al., 2019), it is not unusual to find individuals fluidly joining and leaving conversations on a wide range of topics, such as academic projects, teaching, tutoring, and lives outside of the academy. When I was researching for this section, there happened to be several Kanaka Maoli graduate students in the center, all who have worked with me for some time in different capacities. I mentioned that I could not find the word collaborate in the *Hawaiian Dictionary* (Pukui & Elbert, 1986), and quite unexpectedly, this sparked an ongoing conversation about all the words they knew that captured the concept of collaboration. The exchange did not end when one of the students went to class; as a matter of fact, they came back after class and rejoined the conversation that had waxed, waned, and waxed again. Indeed, it became a conversation that continued over several days. One of the exchanges resulted in us talking about paddling, and how in this activity, individuals play different roles in a collaborative exercise, which, of course, drove me to investigate the example of paddling mentioned earlier. They shared their understanding of different words, often identifying root terms, tracing how it evolved into a current application, and then checking with each other to compare experiences when they recalled the words or phrases used by their kumu and kūpuna (elders). As I write this, I am still inspired by their generosity toward each other as they learned from one another—and their generosity in teaching me and allowing me access. The interchange represents the kind of collaboration I hope to capture here, and highlights that successful collaboration is more than an isolated behavior or activity. It is an attitude and a habit of mind, imbued with respect and generosity.

This experience, like the one that I opened this chapter with, represents the habit of mind—the stance—I am trying to capture when I talk about a theory of collaboration informed by Indigenous ways of knowing and interacting. Generosity and respect play a key role in this worldview, as does reciprocity, along with several other concepts not easily translated into English. But these attributes are not distinct, separate behaviors for Kanaka Maoli—they inform and engender each other. To better depict this interconnectivity, next I draw from how Kanaka Maoli scholars have written on these concepts. I want to stress again the importance of looking to Kanaka Maoli to explain the concepts presented here, rather than me, someone without genealogical ties to the culture, attempting to do so. My goal is to adapt approaches and practices, not claim or re/define them. Thus, all the scholars referred to in this section are Kanaka Maoli unless otherwise noted, and I will look to their work to guide my rendering of these ideas into English, which is no easy task. Larry Kimura (1983) explains, "whenever Hawaiian is translated into English, the English words used add cultural connotations to the idea conveyed, while eliminating intended connotations and meanings of the original Hawaiian" (p. 182). But it is not just the cultural lens embedded in language use that complicates translation. Multiple meanings are often tied to a single concept, which in a Western context might result in ambiguity or confusion. But as Noenoe Silva (2004) illustrates, word play that exploits this multiplicity is not only valued, it is marshaled by Kanaka Maoli as a rhetorical technique:

> Sometimes several of the meanings are intended by the author, and to choose one English word does considerable violence to the text. Further, sometimes it is not perfectly clear from the context which or how many of the possible English glosses come closest to the meaning understood by Hawaiian readers. Writers of Hawaiian, moreover, value multiplicity in meaning and thus often choose words specifically because many meanings can be derived from them.
> (p. 12)

This multiplicity can also act as a kind of check and balance, mediating authority, moderating agency, and foregrounding community participation and responsibility—an effective paradigm when enacting collaboration.

A significant concept that informs almost every aspect of a Kanaka Maoli worldview is kuleana, and it embodies attributes I will argue can engender a heightened awareness of our collaborative acts and their implications. It plays an instrumental role in how individuals interact with each other, 'āina (land), and moana (sea) holistically, and thus can inform a critically conscious and ethical collaboration. There is not an exact translation in English for kuleana, as the first four words used to define it in the *Hawaiian Dictionary* (Pukui & Elbert, 1986), "right, privilege, concern, responsibility," each have very different meanings in English. In terms of application in an academic context, ku'ualoha ho'omanawanui (2014) writes that kuleana mediates both ethos and ethical practice:

> Hawaiian cultural protocols serve as guidelines for research, particularly the value of kuleana (right, responsibility). In academic inquiry, kuleana is applicable to the concept of one's right to information or to share information, as well as one's responsibilities in this knowledge and sharing.
>
> (pp. xiv–xv)

Noelani Goodyear-Ka'ōpua (2015) discusses kuleana in regard to what it means for those conducting Hawaiian studies research, and further affirms the connection the concept has to ethical interactions, noting, "we must always consider our positionality and obligations" (p. 2). While individuals have kuleana to those they interact with as well as the 'āina, both ho'omanawanui and Goodyear-Ka'ōpua underscore that kuleana is shaped by several ethical considerations and that not everyone can and should have the same kuleana. Implicit in their projects is an assumption of affect beyond any immediate context; thus, attending to the possible ramifications of an act is essential. Mehana Vaughan (2018) similarly emphasizes that kuleana is determined by a community for the needs of that community: "In Hawaiian, one word, kuleana, means rights as well as responsibilities. Kuleana is expressed through specific actions or practices that build to create broader impacts when practiced as a community" (p. 6). Kuleana, then, when fully realized goes beyond an individual's actions; it is a dynamic interplay that attends to the concerns and interests of the community.

When I try to apply kuleana to my own undertakings, it captures the idea that a right is also a privilege that automatically corresponds to certain responsibilities and concerns that should be attended to by those with privilege. Kuleana as a concept is profound because it subsumes a variety of behaviors and actions meant to facilitate pono actions that benefit all and maintain balance. The definition of pono in the *Hawaiian Dictionary* (Pukui & Elbert, 1986) is quite long, but key words include goodness, correct, and righteous, but pono is also commonly conceived as representing balance. When invoking pono as a part of a Hawaiian studies research paradigm, Goodyear-Kaʻōpua (2015) explains it as "signifying the search for and maintenance of harmonious relationships, justice, and healing" (pp. 17–18). Marie Alohalani Brown (2016) correlates pono to ethical behavior, describing it as a challenging endeavor that ideally permeates the entirety of one's interactions:

> By 'pono,' I mean that holistic balance we achieve when we are physically, spiritually, morally, and intellectually ethical, and in equilibrium with ourselves, with others, with our ancestors, with our gods, and with the environment (land, sea, and sky)—a challenging goal, but our greatest and most rewarding task.
>
> (p. 158)

A stance informed by these two protocols, kuleana and pono, is infused with generosity, an attribute held in great esteem in a Kanaka Maoli worldview—as Trask (1993) points out, "unstinting generosity is a value and of high status" (p. 187). Along with generosity is respect, a quality that places value on other's knowledge and experience; it encourages us to listen so that others have room to tell their own stories, or enact a task in their own way in their own time; it reminds us of others' rights to be and to have access and agency. And finally, reciprocity is an offshoot of these combined behaviors—to be generous and respectful naturally leads to ensuring mutually beneficial relationships. In her germinal text, *Decolonizing methodologies: Research and Indigenous peoples*, Māori scholar Linda Tuhiwai Smith (1999)[8] explains key elements for researchers in establishing reciprocal relationships with participants and their communities: the interests and concerns of research participants should be heard and engaged; the research should benefit all parties; and the knowledge gained through the research should be disseminated to the community that helped shape it. Smith (1999) grounds the concepts of reciprocity and respect as intrinsic to an Indigenous worldview:

> The term 'respect' is consistently used by indigenous peoples to underscore the significance of our relationships and humanity. Through respect the place of everyone and everything in the universe is kept in balance and harmony. Respect is a reciprocal, shared, constantly interchanging principle which is expressed through all aspects of social conduct.
>
> (p. 120)

Smith here illustrates the interconnectedness of these behaviors and their role in ensuring pono outcomes—highlighting that such work requires looking outward so that the individual is always aware of their position amongst others in a larger social context.

Considering these treatments collectively, I understand from these scholars that before approaching an interaction, contemplation and consideration of the impact of my actions on those I interact with as well as the surrounding environment is necessary. This interconnectivity is what I want to highlight in adapting these concepts. Understanding these concepts as not separate, but rather inseparable, centers ethical behaviors and decenters the practitioner's agenda, so that both potentials and consequences are conceived of more broadly. In other words, the practitioner-researcher's objectives/agendas are secondary to the potential implications on the wider community. One of the students who was involved in the conversation on Kanaka Maoli concepts of collaboration mentioned earlier provided a clear illustration of this dynamic, telling me that in 'ōlelo Hawai'i sentence structure, the action always precedes the actor, highlighting the relative roles between action and actor and the humility expected of the latter.

Conceptualizing Collaboration

As a non-Indigenous person, albeit one who has been fortunate to be influenced by the culture and traditions of Hawai'i, I am conscious of the contradictions between being raised within a larger American settler colonial culture that promotes individualism and learning how to interact with the world in a place that values communal and collaborative interactions. I think of how often I have heard students tell me that collaborations just do not work and are not fair. Sometimes the unwillingness to work as part of a group is justified, but often it can be traced back to a fundamental privilege of individual achievement in American society, especially in the academy. The value placed on individual accomplishment may even play a role in the disparity between actual treatments of collaboration in terms of both theory and practice, and the pervasive invocations of "collaboration" in the scholarship that infer, but often do not define, collaborative practices. From the time many of us are very young, we are often encouraged to collaborate, and it is not too difficult to imagine how this contradicts with individualism promoted in the United States. Thus, the relationship many of us have with collaboration may be slippery—we know it is good when we can do it, but the models for success often held up as example tend to feature solo endeavors. Since collaboration is not an attribute overtly valued in Western ways of knowing and being, it is easy to understand the tendency to reduce collaboration to a set of sometimes vague practices rather than a way of being. Collaboration, however, is more than a set of practices, although that is definitely a part of it. It is an attitude, habit of mind, and, in terms of this project, a critical element of a practitioner's stance (as explained in Chapter 1) in their approach to their work and research. And, it is in the conceptualizing of one's stance that the frameworks discussed in the previous sections can work as a guide.

The idea of collaboration I am proposing is targeted mostly to practitioners who initiate collaborative acts like teachers or writing center directors—whether in research or practice—and also those they engage with in such endeavors, such as students, writing center consultants, and research participants. Enacting collaboration in this frame demands transparent and productive discussion with all participants to engender reflexivity in terms of individual positions and power dynamics with the goal of creating space for all voices to be heard, but especially for those who have experiences of being silenced, whether at the societal level, in the academy and classroom, or due to personal circumstances. Doing so does not mean we need to assume someone's marginalization or that participants need to disclose sensitive information; what it means is interlocutors need to be sensitive to other's ways of communicating and respect them.

While the model proposed here builds on the work of writing studies and education scholars who have articulated theories of collaboration (Bruffee, 1984; Trimbur, 1989; Ede & Lunsford, 1992; Cochran-Smith & Lytle, 2009), and those who contributed to understandings of ethical research practices (Kirsch & Ritchie, 1995), it does so by adapting the approaches I discuss in the previous section, so they are applicable to research, practice, and pedagogy in writing centers, writing studies, and related fields. In adapting kuleana and pono, to these contexts, I begin with the premise that occupying the position of practitioner-researcher is a privilege that comes with responsibility to not only our teaching, research, and service, but also to the consultants, writers, and colleagues we work with as well as the institutions we work within and the places where they are located. An underlying principle in such an endeavor is that it should be ethical and undertaken with generosity and respect for all participants, the work itself, and the place in which it is enacted. How—and how much—reciprocity is realized by not only participants but also by our larger environment and community should also be attended to. A stance informed by these concepts foregrounds inclusion, with a practitioner recursively reflecting on ways to welcome all who have a stake in the endeavor at hand. The following tenets are designed to ground a collaborative act. They are informed by my understandings of these Kanaka Maoli approaches, limited as it is by my positioning as a non-Indigenous ally. Thus, I do not refer to the concepts by their name in ʻōlelo Hawaiʻi in these articulations to emphasize that these are adaptations, and to avoid any inference that what I present here is sufficient to fully grasp what it means to live by and through these concepts. Each tenet is followed by a set of questions for identifying the extent to which it is realized, which is then followed by a short explanation of the reasoning for the tenet.

Tenets for a Practitioner's Collaborative Stance

- The structure and objective of a collaborative act should first be discussed with all participants before tackling the task at hand.
  - Questions: Who are the participants? What are their respective roles? What is the objective, both in terms of end product and in-process learning?
  - Explanation: Transparency, even when it reveals uncomfortable underpinnings (i.e., in terms of positionality or objectives), gets us closer to collaboration than masking them does.
- Collaboration is not a zero-sum game; it occurs on a continuum. We should be conscious of where on the continuum a collaborative act lies.
  - Questions: How much control does/must a facilitator exert? How are the participants responding to the group dynamics? Who is doing what work? And how do those efforts and corresponding benefits compare?
  - Explanation: Sometimes the structure is decided by the person "in charge," like the teacher or administrator. That does not necessarily make an interaction non-collaborative, but in such a scenario or others like it, the elements of the interaction that are not collaborative should be identified.
- Concerns/interests of all participants should be considered and addressed to the extent possible.

What Indigenous Practices Can Teach Us   49

- Questions: What does each participant hope to gain out of the interaction? How do these agendas compare? Can all interests be attended to? If not, are their compromises?
  - Explanation: Again, this comes down to transparency, and, in this case, it facilitates attending to different interests and concerns, which promotes learning, realization of benefits, and also purposeful engagement.
- In a collaborative act, participants (definitely facilitators, but also other participants) should reflect on their own positionality within and in relation to the larger group, with the goal of recognizing skills, talents, or even shortcomings one brings to the interaction as well as actual or perceived privilege.
  - Questions: What privilege do I bring with me (my situated ethos)? What is the group dynamic and how are others responding to me? What does each participant bring (i.e., skills, knowledge, experience)? Does everyone have space to contribute/benefit? How am I responding to other's knowledge and contributions?
  - Explanation: Sometimes, a basic question like who is talking most or giving the most directions can provide insight here. The objective of practicing reflexivity is to first become aware of our own roles and how our interactions may be received, and then to gain an understanding of whether adjustments to our interactional style can create a more balanced dynamic.
- The ideal goal of a collaborative act is that it promotes reciprocity—all participants should benefit in comparable ways, with the impact on the community and the environment also considered in terms of reciprocity.
  - Questions: What am I getting out of/contributing to this interaction? What are other participants getting out of/contributing to this interaction? How does what I am gaining/giving compare to what other participants are gaining/giving? What is the wider-reaching impact of my work on the community and place we are in?
  - Explanation: Participants should remain aware of how everyone involved is or is not benefiting and what each member is contributing. There may be situations where some do not benefit or do not benefit in comparable ways. That is likely unavoidable and should be acknowledged, but efforts should also be made to mitigate disparities in reciprocity.
- All participants should respect their collaborators.
  - Questions: What skill/talent/knowledge do my collaborators bring to the table that I do not? What are my strengths? What are my weaknesses? How do the attributes of my collaborators

compensate for any of my shortcomings in terms of what can be done, how it is done, and what is known or understood?
- Explanation: The experiences and knowledge of each participant should be acknowledged and respected. Space should be provided for each participant's knowledge and experiences to be engaged, understanding that sometimes communication styles prevent applicability from being immediately apparent. Listening, hearing, and patience must all be exercised.
- Attend to the context in which the collaborative act takes place, to the extent possible.
  - Questions: What is our social/historical/cultural context? To what extent does where this interaction takes place impact the interaction? Does it impact participants in different ways? What ways, if any, does this interaction impact our "place"?
  - Explanation: Our interactions do not occur in a vacuum, and just as we are influenced by our politics of place, our actions and interactions likewise impact our social/political/geographic spheres of practice. We should attend to how our work impacts wider communities, even if it is simply in terms of the individuals leaving our locations and returning to their communities with new information.

Following these tenets pushes us to discuss what is expected when we assign collaborative activities in classrooms, as part of training, or claiming collaboration in our research. We should be clear about the expected outcomes *vis-à-vis* the collaborative interaction; in other words, what role is collaborating expected to play? A collaborative interaction should provide space for each participant to contribute. Doing so necessitates acknowledging each participant's knowledge and the value of that knowledge in successfully navigating the task at hand. In classroom settings in particular, a facilitator, often the teacher, must also consider how each group member is experiencing a collaborative assignment. The facilitator must always be mindful of their accountability to participants and work to engender some level of accountability amongst participants. When one participant is not experiencing the interaction as collaborative, the facilitator should reflect on whether any intervention or adjustment to the exercise or group dynamic can mediate the disparity in experience. Participant-participant accountability will vary depending on the length of the interaction. In a classroom exercise for example, it can manifest in the simple good will evidenced by active engagement.

The common thread that runs throughout the tenets and questions laid out here is reflexivity. Ultimately, an ethical collaboration requires that all participants reflect critically on positionality and the impact of their actions on their fellow collaborators, the work at hand, and the place in which it is undertaken. This approach moves away from an outcome-driven perspective to one focused on process and the journey. It is informed by a Kanaka Maoli worldview that emphasizes connectivity and imbues the positions we occupy with rights, privileges, and responsibilities, a singular concept in which the three cannot be separated.

Conclusion

Andrea Lunsford (1991) got it right when she proclaimed, "creating a collaborative environment and truly collaborative tasks is damnably difficult" (p. 3). Collaboration is hard in that it demands us to critically reflect on our own power, how it is wielded, and what is at stake in terms of our own personal gain or benefit when we exercise that power. And it becomes even harder when a set of tenets to guide such endeavors is not there. If we think of collaboration as occurring on a continuum, then the range of what counts as collaboration is quite vast, and determining the point of a collaborative act on that continuum necessitates a critical lens. The goal of this chapter was to provide tenets to inform such a critical lens, and I looked to Kanaka Maoli approaches to guide this work precisely because the values embedded in concepts that inform their worldview, as I have argued, can further our own understandings of collaboration. The following chapters illustrate what collaboration as articulated here can "look" like in research, teaching, and practice. Obviously, not every tenet is applicable in every situation, nor am I suggesting that if you follow these tenets you will achieve some utopian ideal of collaboration. Rather, what I hope my contribution does offer is a means to assess a collaborative act, to move away from the binary of collaboration either did or did not happen, toward a more critical stance that promotes understanding of how and the extent to which collaboration was realized by all participants.

Notes

1 I use practitioner here and throughout as it is defined in the Introduction to this volume.
2 Both Hawaiian and Native Hawaiian are used to refer to the Indigenous people of Hawai'i.

3 As I will explain in a later section, many Hawaiian words cannot be reduced through translation into a single English word without loosing significant attributes. Kumu is one such word. It is commonly translated as teacher, but it also encompasses concepts like source, model, example, motive, and foundation (Pukui & Elbert, 1986, p. 182), indicating when someone is designated as kumu, their role is much more holistic.
4 I am intentionally choosing not to cite here as these kinds of invocations are too common, and identifying a specific work would belie the pervasiveness of such constructs.
5 There are definitions of collaboration that point to working as a spy or traitor to one's country; however, I do not feel those are directly relevant to the discussion at hand.
6 As I will discuss further later in this section, in many cases, Hawaiian words have multiple meanings, which allows for the word play common in Kanaka Maoli oral traditions. Because of space constraints, in all the definitions I provide, I have left several alternative definitions out, some of which ground these acts with specific activities, like working in a kalo patch.
7 In Hawai'i, paddling is a traditional cultural practice, which has resulted in it being very popular contemporary competitive sport.
8 Linda Tuhiwai Smith's work articulating Indigenous research methdologies has been widely influential. Moreover, as a Māori scholar, her work is particularly relevant to the discussion here as the Māori have familial ties to Kanaka Maoli as Indigenous people of the Pacific and share many values, protocols, and traditions.

References

Brown, M. A. (2016). *Facing the spears of change: The life and legacy of john Papa 'I'i*. Honolulu: University of Hawai'i Press.

Bruffee, K. (1984). Collaborative learning and the "conversation of mankind". *College English, 46*(7), 635–652.

Cochran-Smith, M., & Lytle, S. (2009). *Inquiry as stance: Practitioner research for the next generation*. New York, NY: Teachers College Press.

Duffy, W. (2014). Collaboration (in) theory: Reworking the social turn's conversational imperative. *College English, 76*(5), 416–435.

Etymonline. (2020). Collaboration. In *Online Etymology Dictionary*. Retrieved from https://www.etymonline.com/search?q=collaboration

Goodyear-Ka'ōpua, N. (2015). Reproducing the ropes of resistance: Hawaiian studies methodologies. In K. R. K. N. Oliveira & E. K. Wright (Eds.), *Kanaka 'Oiwi Methodologies* (pp. 1–29). Honolulu: University of Hawai'i Press.

ho'omanawanui, k. (2014). *Voices of fire: Reweaving the literary lei of Pele and Hi'iaka*. Minneapolis: University of Minnesota Press.

Hurley, T. (2020, March 3). "After over a century in England, 20 native Hawaiian skulls return home to Hawaii." *StarAdvertiser*. Retrieved March 3, 2020, from https://www.staradvertiser.com/2020/03/03/hawaii-news/20-native-

hawaiian-skulls-are-returned-from-england/?HSA=2d6f4f865fd199134e-3cac0a7298c4965aaff3f4
Kimura, L. (1983). "Native Hawaiian culture." In United States Native Hawaiian Study Commission (Ed.), *Report on the culture, needs and concerns of Native Hawaiians pursuant to Public Law 96–565, Title III* (pp. 173–224). Washington, DC: The Commission.
Kirsch, G., & Ritchie, J. (1995). Beyond the personal: Theorizing a politics of location in composition research. *College Composition and Communication, 46*(1), 7–29.
Lanikai Canoe Club. (2020). The crews. *Lanikai Canoe Club.* Retrieved from https://lanikaicanoeclub.org/members-info/
Liggett, S., Jordan, K., & Price, S. (2011). Mapping knowledge-making in writing center research: A taxonomy of methodologies. *Writing Center Journal, 31*(2), 50–88.
Lunsford, A. (1991). Collaboration, control, and the idea of a writing center. *The Writing Center Journal, 12*(1), 3–10.
Lunsford, A., & Ede, L. (1992). *Singular texts/plural authors. Perspectives on collaborative writing.* Carbondale: Southern Illinois University Press.
McDougall, B. (2010). *The salt-wind: Ka makani pa'akai.* Honolulu, HI: Kuleana 'Ōiwi Press.
Merriam-Webster. (2020). Collaboration. In *Merriam-Webster.com dictionary.* Retrieved from https://www.merriam-webster.com/dictionary/collaboration
Meyer, M. A. (2001). Our own liberation: Reflections on Hawaiian epistemology. *Contemporary Pacific, 13*(1), 124–148.
Nordstrom, G., Furtado, N., Gushiken, G., Ito-Fujita, A., Iwashita, K., Kurashige, N., Togafau, K., & Wang, I. (Fall 2019). Affirming our liminality & writing on the walls: How we welcome in our writing center. *The Peer Review Journal, 3*(1). Retrieved June 1, 2020 from http://thepeerreview-iwca.org/issues/redefining-welcome/affirming-our-liminality-writing-on-the-walls-how-we-welcome-in-our-writing-center/
Pratt, M. (2008). *Imperial eyes: Travel writing and transculturation* (2nd ed.). New York, NY: Routledge.
Pukui, M. K. (1983). *'Ōlelo no'eau: Hawaiian proverbs & poetical sayings.* Honolulu, HI: Bishop Museum Press.
Pukui, M. K., & Elbert, S. H. (1986). *Hawaiian dictionary.* Honolulu: University of Hawai'i Press.
Silva, N. K. (2004). *Aloha betrayed: Native Hawaiian resistance to American colonialism.* Durham, NC: Duke University Press.
Smith, L. T. (1999). *Decolonizing methodologies: Research and indigenous peoples.* New York, NY: Zed Books.
Trask, H. K. (1993). *From a native daughter: Colonialism and sovereignty in Hawai'i.* Monroe, ME: Common Courage Press.
Trask, H. K. (1999). *Light in the crevice never seen* (Rev. ed.). Corvallis, OR: Calyx Books.

Trimbur, J. (1989). Consensus and difference in collaborative learning. *College English, 51*(6), 602–616.

Vaughan, M. B. (2018). *Kaiaulu: Gathering tides.* Corvallis: Oregon State University Press.

WAC Clearinghouse. (2020). Collaboration. In *CompPile*. Retrieved from https://wac.colostate.edu/comppile/

2 Practitioner Inquiry
A Model for Research and Practice in the Writing Center

This project is grounded primarily in writing center studies; however, the model I present in this chapter is also appropriate for other educational contexts, including composition classrooms as well as other learning support contexts. Indeed, my own introduction to Practitioner Inquiry began with my dissertation work, with an empirical investigation conducted in two composition classes. That project was born as a response to attitudes and stereotypes I have heard all my life—that "local" students[1] are underprepared for academia, with "cannot be prepared" sometimes remaining an unspoken subtext, but too often part of the verbalized discourse. Frequently, our Pidgin language,[2] or Hawai'i Creole, is noted as one of the root causes, but as the most common speakers of the language are Kanaka Maoli (Hawaiian), and descendants of the mostly Asian laborers brought to the islands to work on the plantations, these sentiments are often drawn along racial lines. Common misrepresentations about students' intellect are derived from some students not actively engaging in class discussions or not responding in the expected way to teacher's "treatments," expectations that often presuppose a response grounded in EuroAmerican norms. The irony here is that I am not a member of one of the aforementioned ethnicities, I am Italian American, and often I am mistaken for coming from the continental US, despite that I identify as being of this place. My appearance has resulted in people expressing to me their disregard for our language and racist ideas about people in my community, not realizing my position as a member of this community. I designed my dissertation to capture the savvy ways local students enact critical literacy practices that can go undetected by people not from here.

The goal of the project was to assemble a corpus of data that countered those harmful perceptions, but early on I realized I needed a methodology that foregrounds empowering research participants, provides space for them to tell their stories, and assumes all participants in an engagement bring experience and knowledge to the exchange. I also knew that while I recognize the inaccuracies and harm of such stereotypes circulating in our public discourse and have witnessed their damaging effects, I do not fully get how these stereotypes are experienced. Simply because I present as a "white" person who easily uses standard American English when it suits my purpose, I have not experienced being prejudged as not being intellectually prepared. I thus needed a methodology that reminded me to approach my data through what Barney Glaser & Anslem Strauss (1967) term "grounded theory," a practice wherein rather than looking for data to prove or disprove a theory (which I would necessarily already have to be aware of), the researcher allows theory to emerge from the data. In other words, in engaging with data, the researcher is always open to recognizing something they did not expect, or account for variables they may not have previously identified. Approaching the data in this way was primary to this project because I knew I could not anticipate all the ways in which students in these classrooms were critically engaging in their writing. I also needed a methodology that provided a framework for working with my students as coresearchers because, to come close to constructing an accurate representation of their experiences, I needed them to tell me what they could see that I could not. Teacher-research, the forerunner to Practitioner Inquiry, fits the bill. One of the attractions of teacher-research was that it provided a framework for teaching praxis as well as practices that are part of the actual research so that a practitioner's full context can be accounted for.

Several years later, when I began conducting research as a writing center director, I again needed a methodology to guide my empirical research with all the same criteria I had outlined in my previous study. Certain elements of the research context were a little bit different, however. I was not exactly a teacher, and, in some ways different than in the classroom setting, the consultants I trained and worked with have knowledge and experience essential to fully capture writing center exchanges. By that time, scholars working in teacher-research had pointed out that this approach worked for other kinds of practitioners working in educational contexts—which for me meant practitioners like writing center directors. Through my PhD work, I knew that teacher-research encompassed practices meant to realize key aspects of empirical research, such as systematicity, validity, and veracity. For the scholars ushering the transition to Practitioner Inquiry, all the same rigors remained in place. I quickly realized, however,

Practitioner Inquiry had not been dealt with the same consistency or as robustly in writing center studies. That is where the story of the model explicated in this chapter begins.

Practitioner Inquiry: Commonalities and Limitations in Existing Models

As discussed in the Introduction to this book, treatments of Practitioner Inquiry in writing center studies are varied and inconsistent in terms of documenting its rigor. Sarah Liggett, Kerri Jordan, & Steve Price (2011) provide one of the most thorough explications of Practitioner Inquiry as it is practiced in the field in "Mapping Knowledge-Making in Writing Center Research: A Taxonomy of Methodologies." Their extended examination of Practitioner Inquiry specifically within writing center studies makes it an appropriate departure point in my efforts to articulate it as a research model for this field. Table 2.1 provides excerpts from their discussion of Practitioner Inquiry and aligns them with Marilyn Cochran-Smith & Susan Lytle's (2009) "Common Characteristics" of Practitioner Inquiry (written in italics in Table 2.1). In the sections that follow, I will first discuss the commonalities between the two models—both those that are apparent and those that are implicated in discussion. Then, I will explain the limitations, noting how further articulation in terms of methodology with method is necessary to build a research model applicable and replicable across writing center sites so as to lay the groundwork for the last section of this chapter in which I will present a complete Practitioner Inquiry research model.[3]

Commonalities

The first six characteristics named by Cochran-Smith & Lytle (2009) (Table 2.1) align closely not only with Liggett, Jordan, & Price's (2011) discussion of Practitioner Inquiry, but with writing center pedagogy in general. Many of these features, such as *Practitioner as Researcher* (Table 2.1, #1) and *Professional Context as Inquiry Site/Professional Practice as Focus of Study* (Table 2.1, #2), are similarly hallmarks to Practitioner Inquiry as practiced in writing center research. And these first two characteristics are intricately related to a specific habit of mind enacted regularly by writing center practitioners: Cochran-Smith & Lytle (2009) call it "inquiry as stance," whereas Liggett, Jordan, & Price (2011) name it "reflexive stance," noting it is

58   *Practitioner Inquiry*

Table 2.1 Comparison of Practitioner Inquiry Models from Education and Writing Center Studies

Cochran-Smith & Lytle (2009) Common Characteristics of Practitioner Inquiry	Liggett, Jordan, & Price (2011) Corresponding Characteristics of Practitioner Inquiry
1 Practitioner as researcher: "the practitioner himself or herself simultaneously takes on the role of researcher" (p. 41).	"Those who engage in Practitioner Inquiry … may be administrators, teachers, or peer tutors, but they are also writers." (p. 56).
2 Professional context as inquiry site/professional practice as focus of study: "the professional context is taken as the site for inquiry, and problems and issues that arise from professional practice are the focus of study" (p. 42).	"Since working with writers one-on-one remains the primary *modus operandi* of writing centers, [Stephen] North identifies this context as the 'most obvious setting' for Practitioner Inquiry: it is where problems find tutors in the writing center" (p. 57). "Pragmatic Inquiry [a sub-category of Practitioner Inquiry] usually begins with a local, practice-related experience or observation that prompts the Practitioner to engage in research …" (p. 61).
3 Community and collaboration: "Although some practitioner research is conducted by individuals, collaboration among and across participants is a key feature" (p. 41).	Collaboration is implicated through the important role placed on dialectic exchange that entails, for example, "engaging in discussion with others (such as tutors, student writers, administrators, teachers, and writing center directors)" (p. 62).
4 Assumptions about links of knowledge, knowers, and knowing: "the assumption that those who work in a particular educational context and/or who live in particular social situations have significant knowledge about those situations" (p. 42).	"our community has long valued the experiential knowledge of practitioners" (p. 54).
5 Blurred boundaries between inquiry and practice: "The boundaries between inquiry and practice blur when the practitioner is researcher and the professional context is a site for research" (pp. 42–43).	"Practitioner Inquiry, then, is reflexive, experientially based research that relies on dialectic [inquiry] to examine experience [practice] and to arrive at carefully investigated and tested personal knowledge" (p. 58).

Cochran-Smith & Lytle (2009) Common Characteristics of Practitioner Inquiry	Liggett, Jordan, & Price (2011) Corresponding Characteristics of Practitioner Inquiry
6 Publicity, public knowledge, and critique: "Most descriptions of Practitioner Inquiry emphasize making the work public and open to the critique of a larger community" (pp. 44–50).	"Practitioner Inquirers contribute significantly to our research community: they offer knowledge against which other Practitioners test and validate their own understanding, and they publish and present studies that become springboards" (p. 59).
7 New conceptions of validity and generalizability: "notions of validity and generalizability are quite different from the traditional criteria" (p. 43).	Validity: "Practitioner Inquirers employ reflexive, dialectical means to test and validate their work" (p. 58). Generalizability: "Practitioner Inquirers overstep methodological boundaries if they attach global implications to their findings" (p. 63).
8 Systematicity including data collection and analysis: "systematic documentation [can] resemble the forms of data collection used in other qualitative studies [and] entails multiple data sources that illuminate and confirm but also disconfirm one another" (p. 44).	"Pragmatic Inquiry [a subcategory of Practitioner Inquiry] requires a skeptical eye; the researcher must analyze the problem or issue from a variety of angles, especially those that offer opposing interpretations or positions" (p. 61).

"crucial to the success" of the Practitioner Inquiry methodology for writing center researchers (p. 57).[4] Reflexivity for Liggett, Jordan, & Price (2011) takes on a dialectic form wherein the practitioner continually interrogates and reflects on assumptions and practices within the larger context of experiences and other's knowledge (peers, students, published works, etc.), suggesting a privileging of different knowledge sources and a sense of collaboration in terms of incorporating that knowledge (p. 58). With their term inquiry as stance, Cochran-Smith & Lytle (2009) similarly emphasize reflexivity and perspective but expand their definition to highlight the political nature of such research: "it is social and political in the sense of deliberating about what to get done, why to get it done, who decides, and whose interests are served" (p. 121). Implicit then is that a practitioner embodying this habit of mind constantly interrogates whose knowledge is valued, and their inquiry thus encompasses ways to counter structures of power that privilege certain ways of knowing and being. While Cochran-Smith & Lytle offer a fuller explication of the stance a practitioner inquirer inhabits, this kind of interrogation of knowledge and hierarchies of power are not only inherent to writing center pedagogy, they are at the very foundation of writing center studies. Indeed, early conceptions of writing center work, such as Andrea Lunsford's (1992) "idea of a writing center informed by a theory of knowledge as socially constructed ... that presents a challenge to the institution of higher education" (p. 5), represent the political and disruptive position writing centers can potentially achieve within an institution often mired in constrained ideas about what counts as knowledge and for whom.

Along this same trajectory of breaking with traditional separations between practice and knowledge-making within academia, Cochran-Smith & Lytle (2009) name *Community and Collaboration* (Table 2.1, #3) and *Assumptions about Links of Knowledge, Knowers, and Knowing* (Table 2.1, #4) as essential characteristics of Practitioner Inquiry. Both concepts are implicit in Liggett, Jordan, & Price's (2011) discussion and, like interrogation of hierarchies of power, are foundational to writing center theory. Lunsford (1992), for example, posits conceptions of collaboration and the social construction of knowledge as ingrained in the efforts to dismantle hierarchical power structures. Finally, in terms of *Blurred Boundaries between Inquiry and Practice* (Table 2.1, #5) and *Publicity, Public Knowledge and Critique* (Table 2.1, #6), how these two concepts are actuated in similar ways in both fields seems obvious: the first is an effect of conducting research within one's practice site, with all the benefits and challenges that such a scenario presents; the second is realized in the volume of publications and conferences through which the research is disseminated.

I have renumbered *Validity and Generalizability* and *Systematicity* so they are last on the list because these are the two areas that I believe need the most attention in terms of reformulating methods that facilitate their realization, a discussion I take up in the next section.

Limitations

While the commonalities between the two models of Practitioner Inquiry, particularly in terms of the first six characteristics (as numbered in Table 2.1), might seem quite obvious, what is also clear is that Cochran-Smith & Lytle's (2009) articulation of Practitioner Inquiry more precisely presents as a research model. The authors list eight clearly defined features (theories/approaches) informing the methodology that are shared across genres of Practitioner Inquiry, each with corresponding definitions and/or methods. In the construction of this model, Cochran-Smith & Lytle have the benefit of a long history of teacher researchers working to validate the research conducted in their field within wider academic circles, which could be one explanation for the model's clarity. Scholarly calls in our own field are demanding we make similar moves to formally articulate research models (North, 1984; Gillespie et al., 2002; Babcock & Thonus, 2012; Driscoll & Perdue, 2012) for which one end result will be to produce more empirical writing center research. Liggett, Jordan, & Price's (2011) cohesive discussion of Practitioner Inquiry for writing center practitioners addresses a long overdue need for such an explication in our field and thus lays an essential scholarly foundation for any work that attempts to build a research model based on Practitioner Inquiry—the work I undertake here. One of the first steps involved in achieving that objective is looking at the limitations not only to Practitioner Inquiry as a research model in general, but, specifically in terms of this project, examining its limitations in terms of producing empirical research. In the following, I begin by identifying limitations in terms of achieving empirical research as articulated in writing center scholarship and then examine practices associated with Practitioner Inquiry models in terms of their ability to address these limitations.

Responding specifically to the call for RAD (replicable, aggregable, date-based evidence) research (which, according to Haswell's definition, encompasses empirical research), Dana Driscoll & Sherry Winn Perdue (2012) conducted an extensive survey of scholarship to determine how much of our published work could be considered RAD research. Building on Richard Haswell's (2005) project that called attention to the lack of such research, they designed a rubric based on his table, "Definitions of the categories of RAD and non-RAD" (p. 208). Their rubric areas are meant to facilitate a detailed examination of RAD research as well as "determine in what areas writing center research is strong and in what areas research may be lacking" in terms of producing RAD research (Driscoll & Perdue, 2012, p. 20). While the articles examined do not all employ a Practitioner Inquiry methodology, I began my approach to identifying limitations to Practitioner Inquiry as a model using their rubric. If an area in their rubric was rated low in terms of the number of research articles addressing it, that area became a flag, indicating the possibility that methods that correspond to particular features need to be articulated to ensure it is addressed by a research model.

Driscoll & Perdue (2012) note that the three criteria of their rubric that were most successfully addressed in published writing center research are *Background and Significance, Presentation of Results,* and *Discussion and Implications.* The area receiving the lowest score according to their analysis is *Limitation and Future Work,* followed closely by *Selection of Participants/Texts* and *Method of Analysis.* Many of the Practitioner Inquiry features noted in Table 2.1 by both Cochran-Smith & Lytle (2009) and Liggett, Jordan, & Price (2011) could, but do not necessarily, address one of these specific criteria. I suggest here that this ambiguity arises for two related reasons: (1) conflation between methodology and methods, which results in (2) a lack of detail of methods and their application at different points of the research process.[5] To better illustrate my point here, I revisit Sandra Harding's (1987) definitions of methodology and methods that were presented in the Introduction: methodology "is a theory and analysis of how research does or should proceed" (p. 3), whereas method "is a technique for (or way of proceeding in) gathering evidence" (p. 2). Sometimes, however, the methods (or practices) employed to address a particular methodology (or theoretical frame) are conflated with the methodology itself. When distinction between methodology and method is not clearly articulated, the ways in which a particular method does (or does not as the case may be) address the goals of a methodology are not readily apparent, and researchers can rely on the claims of the methodology without acknowledging ways their practices may have limited its realization.

For example, the methodology underpinning a Practitioner Inquiry research model should be informed by a theory of collaboration—as noted in both Cochran-Smith & Lytle (2009) and Liggett, Jordan, & Price (2011), collaboration in some form is part and parcel of Practitioner Inquiry—and the theoretical frame might necessarily be presented in the methodology as an abstract concept. I might, for example, cite Indigenous theories of collaboration and values that are aligned with it, like privileging the voices and concerns of research participants. Conducting and producing empirical research, however, also entails articulating specific methods if research is to be replicable. When a methodology informed by Indigenous theories of collaboration, to continue with this example, is not described with explication of corresponding methods or practices—what practices were implemented to ensure the agency of research participants and how they were implemented—the arena for interpretation of how collaboration is actuated can become too broad and, in the case of a research model, can undermine its efficacy in terms of application across contexts. Similarly, when incorporating go-to collaborative practices commonly employed in writing classrooms and writing centers—such as working in small groups or restructuring seating arrangements—it is also essential to describe how they are enacted. As more fully discussed in Chapter 1, citing a practice as "collaborative" without identifying goals and methods followed by interrogation into how and whether collaboration was truly achieved renders claims of collaboration hollow.

Interestingly, the areas according to Driscoll & Perdue (2012) needing the most attention are ones requiring methodical and systematic practices (methods) rather than theoretical discussion and analysis (methodology). As many writing center practitioners (like me) received our formal training in English departments, theoretical discussion and analysis is arguably one of our strengths, which is likely why areas like *Background and Significance* and *Discussion and Implications* scored high in Driscoll & Perdue's analysis. As Driscoll & Perdue (2012) note, some of their rubric criteria can be met through organizational style (p. 29)—which might explain why "organization" in terms of research presentation is dictated in the social sciences. A research model designed to meet the demands of empirical research must thus mandate inclusion of a systematic discussion of practices to facilitate incorporation of information necessary to produce this kind of research.

In addition to methodology and methods, a model must also accommodate approaches, some to be determined by the project so that the specifics of the research context are attended to, and some deemed integral to the model but leaving room for variability in terms of how they are realized. Examples of the first kind of approaches would include qualitative, quantitative, and mixed-methods approaches, which could be further actualized through conversation analysis, discourse analysis, and corpus-driven analysis. Examples of the second kind of approaches are those identified by Liggett, Jordan, & Price (2011) as being essential to Practitioner Inquiry, *Reflexivity,* and *Dialectic.* The authors see them as interrelated, defining them as informing the "systematic investigation" practitioner inquirers undertake "to test and validate the knowledge they create" (p. 57). The practitioner inquirer thus employs a method of recursively questioning and comparing assumptions and negations against what others have found (using both quantitative and qualitative data) to determine the validity of their own findings. In other words, researchers do not necessarily proceed in linear fashion, but rather revisit claims and findings as more data are gathered and analyzed. Early assumptions are then reevaluated and often reformulated. While reflexivity remains the approach, it could entail a number of different strategies determined by the individual researcher, such as "engaging in discussion with others (such as consultants, student writers, administrators, teachers, and writing center directors), [as well as] borrowing methods used by Conceptual and Empirical researchers" (2011, p. 62). Reflexivity goes hand-in-hand with dialectic as the latter can be realized through these interactions with multiple and varied data sets which could include textual analysis, fieldwork in the form of interviews or conducting surveys, and professional Listservs.

According to Liggett, Jordan, & Price (2011), the main difference between Practitioner Inquiry and other forms of empirical research, as this practice of recursivity suggests, is that the researcher does not work from a fixed research plan. While reformulating and rethinking the research, including essential elements such as research questions and hypothesis, might be a hallmark of Practitioner Inquiry, I argue this does not mean Practitioner Inquiry cannot produce empirical research. The authors note that "a crucial component [of Practitioner Inquiry] is explication of the dialectic, showing how each encounter with 'an other' complicated, enriched, challenged, or confirmed the researcher's thinking" (p. 62); although this recordation of the thinking and interacting process is essential and meaningful, explicit description of data and how and why it was chosen also needs to be included. Thus, a research model would both accommodate practices of recursivity and dialectic exchange, and, at the same time, facilitate description of data and methods used in data collection.

Out of Cochran-Smith & Lytle eight "characteristics," the two that demand the most consideration in a research model are *Validity and Generalizability* and *Systematicity*. While the authors group validity and generalizability together, they discuss them separately, as I will do. In discussing validity, Cochran-Smith & Lytle (2009) argue that different kinds of data—specifically various forms of qualitative data—should be considered valid data sets, a concept solidly aligned with understandings of data amongst writing center practitioners. Citing other scholars in the field, they note that when relying on qualitative data, "validity rests on concrete examples ... of actual practices presented in enough detail that the relevant community can judge trustworthiness and usefulness" and that criteria for evaluating data include "significance, quality, grounding, and authority" (p. 43). Their first criterion is reminiscent of Clifford Geertz's (1973) concept of "thick description," which became a defining element of ethnography after the interpretive turn. Additionally, these methods are informed by notions of collaboration as is evidenced by Cochran-Smith & Lytle's (2009) articulation of several ideas of validity particularly relevant to Practitioner Inquiry:

democratic validity (honoring the perspectives of all stakeholders), outcome validity (resolving the problems addressed), process validity (using appropriate and adequate research methods and inquiry practices), catalytic validity (deepening the understandings of all participants), and dialogic validity (monitoring analysis through critical and reflective discussion with peers).

(p. 44)

Noteworthy here is the way collaboration as a theoretical approach is embedded overtly in concepts such as democratic validity, catalytic validity, and dialogic validity, and implied in outcome validity and process validity. Dialogic validity also corresponds to Liggett, Jordan, & Price's (2011) notion of reflexive/dialectic. In all these iterations of validity, there remains a need for articulation of methods that attends to the implied collaborative approach to determine the realization of these concepts of validity.

Systematicity, of all the features noted by both groups of scholars, is dealt with in most detail in terms of methods. Cochran-Smith & Lytle (2009) describe methods for actuating systematicity to include "documenting classroom practice and students' learning, [and] systematically document[ing] from the inside perspective their own questions, interpretative frameworks, changes in views over time, dilemmas and recurring themes" (p. 44). This approach to systematicity corresponds with the recursive practices Liggett, Jordan, & Price detail as part of a practitioner's reflexive stance wherein "reflective and dialectical means [are employed] to test and validate the knowledge they create," which they correlate with "systematic investigation" (p. 57). In their discussion of systematicity, Cochran-Smith & Lytle (2009) note, "a strength of Practitioner Inquiry is that it entails multiple data sources that illuminate and confirm, but also disconfirm, one another" (44). While the idea of multiple data sets is implied through the discussion of dialectic in Liggett, Jordan, & Price's (2011) work, to strengthen validity, the necessitation of multiple data sources needs to be emphasized in a research model. Incorporating the concept of triangulation (which I will more fully explain in the next section) in a research design can work to underscore the significance of examining a research variable from multiple perspectives.

The discussion of generalizability, however, for both groups of scholars is problematic. For Cochran-Smith & Lytle (2009), the discussion is limited to advocating for new understandings of what generalizability means; they write, "an important feature shared by many forms of Practitioner Inquiry is that notions of validity and generalizability are quite different from the traditional criteria" (p. 43). While the differences in terms of validity are given a fuller treatment, the discussion on generalizability falls short with what that difference means left under-discussed. For Liggett, Jordan, & Price (2011), "Practitioner Inquirers overstep methodological boundaries if they attach global implications to their findings" (p. 63), and, thus, generalizability does not play a role in their conception of Practitioner Inquiry. I see both of these treatments as limiting and propose that a model for Practitioner Inquiry that is designed to meet the demands of empirical research necessarily incorporates some notion of generalizability, which the model I propose in the next section does. And as I have done in my treatment of them here, because of the importance of generalizability and validity to realizing empirical research, I suggest the two concepts be dealt with separately.

Cochran-Smith & Lytle (2009) and Liggett, Jordan, & Price (2011) have contributed significantly to current understandings of Practitioner Inquiry, particularly in explicating essential methodological components and laying groundwork in terms of methods; however, if Practitioner Inquiry is to be presented as a viable research model for producing empirical research, both models need further development. Specifically, an operable model should account for approaches that address the primary concerns of the methodology (i.e., supporting social-constructed knowledge-making practices and collaboration), and then emphasize articulating methods for each point in the research process.

A Model of Practitioner Inquiry for Writing Center Research

As the saying goes, "if it isn't broke, don't fix it," and indeed there are many aspects of Practitioner Inquiry as articulated by Cochran-Smith & Lytle (2009) and Liggett, Jordan, & Price (2011) that are foundational—in short, much of what we currently do when conducting research categorized as Practitioner Inquiry already works. In this section, I present a Practitioner Inquiry Research Model that encompasses elements from these models, noting how this new model builds upon the previous work through adaptations and additions. Before continuing, it is important to note that in the model I present, there is room to account for variability across sites and research foci by incorporating theories that make sense in individual contexts (i.e., feminist theory, queer theory). In my own case, as the discussion in Chapter 1 and in the opening of this chapter points to, my site of practice and research has been significantly impacted by imperial expansion and corresponding colonization. To counter hegemonic constructs in research, I look to Indigenous scholars who have mapped out theories that foreground ways of knowing and being in nations that were once sovereign in order to reposition marginalized epistemologies so they are *at minimum* acknowledged as legitimate, but ideally engaged with equally or even privileged.

Several of the features discussed by both Cochran-Smith & Lytle (2009) and Liggett, Jordan, & Price (2011), such as *Practitioner as Researcher, Professional Context as Inquiry Site/Professional Practice as Focus of Study* and *Blurred Boundaries between Inquiry and Practice*, are identifying characteristics of Practitioner Inquiry and should be incorporated into any Practitioner Inquiry research model. In the model I present here, they will fall under the category of "Determining Factors"—factors to consider when deciding whether a Practitioner Inquiry research model is appropriate for a particular research context.

Theories of collaboration and understanding knowledge as socially constructed, which are identified by Cochran-Smith & Lytle (2009), also need to be integrated. Although these features of Practitioner Inquiry are not specifically named by Liggett, Jordan, & Price (2011), as I have noted earlier, they are implicated in their work and foundational to writing center pedagogy. I would argue, for example, that the dialectic process Liggett, Jordan, & Price (2011) discuss, through which the researcher interrogates their own assumptions and conclusions by interacting with others either directly or through data and scholarship, reflects a valuing of other's knowledge by the very act of incorporating it into the knowledge-making process. I consider collaboration and social construction of knowledge and knowledge-making as theories informing the methodology and guiding practice; thus, methods must be articulated to enhance the realization of them. The specific constructs a practitioner draws from to inform their approach to collaboration is, as I have noted earlier, individual. The treatment of collaboration I provide in Chapter 1, with theoretical grounding and corresponding tenets, informs how I practice it.

In terms of validity (which I propose be separated from generalizability), both groups of scholars include qualitative sources as data and mention making use of multiple data sources to support conjectures. The privileging of qualitative forms of data needs little defense any longer, as even in the sciences, particularly in the area of Science Education, qualitative data play an increasingly prominent role in research (Devetak, Glažar, & Vogrinc, 2010). Liggett, Jordan, & Price's

(2011) notion of dialectic and reflexivity facilitates engaging with multiple data sources in that a practitioner inquirer is constantly looking to others to substantiate or challenge assumptions. Cochran-Smith & Lytle (2009) are more concrete, specifically noting that engagement with multiple data sets is a strength of Practitioner Inquiry. *Triangulation* is the approach advocated for dealing with multiple data sets as a means of strengthening the validity of qualitative research (Miles & Huberman, 1984; Berg, 2001). Validity is undoubtedly enhanced by triangulation, but in actuality, triangulation is more complex than incorporating multiple data sources. Pointing to an understanding of triangulation that expands beyond including multiple data sources, Bruce Berg (2001) notes that "triangulation actually represents varieties of data, investigators, theories, and methods" (p. 4). Thus, embedded in the model I present here, I emphasize triangulation as an element of the methodological approach to be accounted for through engagement with multiple *and* varied kinds of data.

Systematicity is also essential to a research model, and, as discussed previously, both groups of scholars provide some detail as to how systematicity is achieved. Liggett, Jordan, & Price (2011) call for thick description of practices and processes, and Cochran-Smith & Lytle (2009) note the recordation of specific pieces of data such as, classroom activities, learning achieved, thinking processes, etc. The work of these scholars can be used as a springboard to further articulate how and when systematic recordation can enhance empirical research in writing centers, for example, through detailed description of the center site, consultant training practices, consultant-writer/consultant-consultant/consultant-director interactions, and so forth.

This brings me to generalizability. As noted earlier, Liggett, Jordan, & Price (2011) suggest that generalizability lies beyond the scope of Practitioner Inquiry, while Cochran-Smith & Lytle (2009) indicate that it can be achieved, but differently from traditional understandings of research. Both groups of scholars indicate that the inherent aspects of Practitioner Inquiry problematize generalizability—if the research is localized, how can it be generalizable? Although I believe there are instances when Practitioner Inquiry can yield results that are generalizable, I posit the concept of *transferability*, which has been adopted in the field of ethnography, better suits the purposes of a writing center research model. In their overview of *Generalizability and Transferability*, Barnes et al. (1994–2012) explain the two as follows: *Generalizability* "can be defined as the extension of research findings and conclusions from a study conducted on a sample population to the population at large," whereas *Transferability* "does not involve broad claims, but invites readers of research to make connections between elements of a study and their own experience." Transferability provides a frame for validating and making use of our research in a way that more readily lends itself to empirical research in our field. Barnes et al. (1994–2012) explain that transferability facilitates the receivers' agency over determining the applicability of research, noting, "Transferability is a process performed by *readers* of research." For example, to determine transferability, readers note features in the research that are recognizable and comparable to their own. Through thick description, the researcher must supply enough detail for readers to decide whether sufficient similarities exist to determine if the research would produce significant findings if it were undertaken in their own context. The authors go on to note that while transferability can be applied to any kind of research, it is most "relevant" when applied to research involving qualitative data, including ethnographies, case studies, and surveys—all notably common in writing center research and viable within a Practitioner Inquiry framework.

This idea of transferability is not inferior to generalizability; rather, it accounts for the differences that people—students, administrators, faculty, writers, practitioners—bring to a practice site. It represents a dynamism and fluidity, not to be confused with overly specified results that render findings meaningless. Scholars, including those discussed in this chapter, have noted the limitations of Practitioner Inquiry to produce generalizable results; however, as these same and many other scholars argue, the results we produce are valuable and applicable in other contexts. For example, a study I conduct at my center examining how non-dominant languages are mobilized in the center might be duplicated at a different center and yield different results. This difference, however, does not trivialize the results—it can tell us a lot about how different demographics of students engage with non-dominant languages, or it could lead to the identification of practices that promote translanguaging. A multiple site study like this can also tell us important information about how we are normed to certain values, no matter what the context is.

Following is an articulation of a Practitioner Inquiry research model incorporating the elements from the various scholarship I have cited throughout this work. These theories and approaches, such as collaboration, systematicity, triangulation, validity, and transferability, collectively inform both methodology and, correspondingly, the methods necessary for a research model, especially one designed to produce empirical research. One could argue this model is a hybrid, and that may be true insofar as the model incorporates efficacious practices from other preexisting models. In light of the discussion presented here, I have not departed from previously stated understandings of Practitioner Inquiry in significant ways; rather, I have built upon existing models. Only in the case of generalizability have I suggested an entirely new practice in transferability so as bolster our ability to address elements of empirical investigation, such as limitations and implications for future work.

Practitioner Inquiry: An Empirical Research Model

Determining Factors: Both of the following criteria must be met for Practitioner Inquiry to be applicable.

1 *Practitioner as Researcher*: a practitioner in a particular context simultaneously assumes the role of researcher.
2 *Professional Context as Inquiry Site/Professional Practice as Focus of Study*: research is located in/based on the particular context in which a practitioner works. The researcher seeks to answer a

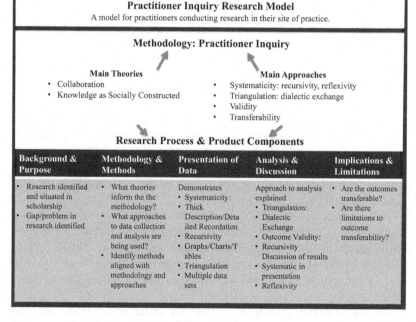

Figure 2.1 Practitioner Inquiry Research Model.

question, solve a problem, and/or improve/identify practices specifically related to the context of their work as a practitioner.

Theories informing Practitioner Inquiry Methodology: The practitioner, when articulating the theoretical underpinnings to their methodology, should consider theories of collaboration to support the social construction of knowledge in an effort to attend to the concerns of all participants.

1   *Collaboration and Social Construction of Knowledge:* The methodology incorporates concepts of collaboration to address the foundational tenets of writing center pedagogy (or the pedagogy aligned with the educational context) and conducting ethical research. Māori scholar, Linda Tuhiwai Smith (1999), explains that respect of participants manifests through a methodology that assumes "people know and can reflect on their own lives, have questions and priorities of their own, have skills and sensitivities which can enhance (or undermine) any community-based projects" (p. 127), all of which should be attended to the extent possible.

Approaches Informing Practitioner Inquiry Methodology: While a practitioner may incorporate other approaches, the following four must be included in any empirical investigation.

1   Systematicity: Thick description and uniformity in presentation of information so that processes are replicable; adopting recursivity as part of systematic processes.
2   Triangulation: Multiple data identified and the way they are operationalized explained; engaging in dialectic with different sources.
3   Validity: How validity is determined is explained (for example, through triangulation).
4   Transferability: How and when might the research be applicable to another site; the limitations of transferability identified.

Essential Components to Research Process and Product: Studies should include sections addressing the following.[6]

1   Background and purpose: Subject of research clearly identified and situated within scholarship; gap/problem in the research identified.
2   Methodology and methods: Research methodology clearly explained and grounded in scholarship (theories and approaches—do they align with an existing model? Or have modifications

been implemented? If so, how and why?) and methods (practices) aligned with methodology articulated. Research subject and/or participants, processes of data collection, and evaluative measures explained. Multiple data sources identified as well as the way they are operationalized (particularly for qualitative data sets) are addressed so that *systematicity* and *validity* are apparent.
3. Presentation of data: Demonstrates (a) *systematicity* through detailed explication, and/or graphs, charts, and tables when relevant; and (b) *triangulation* through identification of multiple data sets.
4. Analysis and discussion: Approach to analysis explained, with focus on *systematicity*; *triangulation* practices implemented to strengthen *validity*: *recursivity* and *dialectic exchange* as tools for analysis. Discussion of results.
5. Implications and limitations: In what ways is the research *transferrable*? Are there considerations/limitations to be taken into account when transferring results?

Conclusion

Practitioner Inquiry is noted as a commonly employed practice in writing center research simply because it facilitates investigations we find most useful and practical: research on how to improve the work we do in the location we do it, whether that be through textual analysis, case study, or a mixed-methods approaches. It seems only logical that if we are to address a call to articulate models for producing empirical research, we first examine the applicability of practices we are already employing. By building upon the foundational work identifying hallmarks of Practitioner Inquiry and its limitations, I have presented a model incorporating concepts of triangulation and transferability, which I suggest can promote the potential of Practitioner Inquiry to produce empirical research. Documenting the efficacy of our practices and then codifying them will be increasingly important if writing centers are to change and adapt to new formulations of academia without losing their identifying characteristics as places that disrupt the hierarchies at work in our institutions. Incorporating elements such as triangulation and transferability into existing iterations of Practitioner Inquiry can facilitate meeting the demands of research—like calls for empirical investigations—while still enacting a hands-on approach that allows us to never lose sight of the theoretical underpinnings—collaboration, the social construction of knowledge, and the corresponding interrogation of hierarchical knowledge structures—that inform our work.

Notes

1 Local is a highly contested term in Hawai'i, with scholars working in settler colonialism highlighting how it has been employed to mask complicitness through claims to Indigenous lands and shared histories. For a more complete treatment of this complex topic, see *Asian settler colonialism: From local governance to the habits of everyday life in Hawai'i* (Fujikane & Okamura, 2008), *Beyond ethnicity: New politics of race in Hawai'i* (Fojas, Gueverra, & Shamar, 2018), *Staking claim: Settler colonialism and racialization in Hawai'i* (Rohrer, 2016).
2 Since Pidgin is the common name for our language and used to refer to it by most speakers, I will refer to it as Pidgin rather than Hawai'i Creole English.
3 For the sake of clarity in the ensuing discussion, I have taken liberty in both reordering Cochran-Smith & Lytle's (2009) presentation of their Practitioner Inquiry characteristics and numbering them.
4 I offer a fuller explanation of stance in the Introduction.
5 It is important to note that sometimes these essential details are left out of articles due to space constraints. Defining a model for such research will hopefully also work to address this issue to some degree.
6 Of course, securing Institutional Review Board approval to research human subjects when appropriate is also an essential part of this process.

References

Babcock, R. D., & Thonus, T. (2012). *Researching the writing center: Towards an evidence-based practice.* New York, NY: Peter Lang Publishing Inc.

Barnes, J., Conrad, K., Demont-Heinrich, C., Graziano, M., Kowalski, D., Neufeld, J., Zamora, J., & Palmquist, M. (1994–2012). Generalizability and Transferability. *Writing@CSU*. Colorado State University. Retrieved January 20, 2019 from http://writing.colostate.edu/guides/guide.cfm?guideid=65.

Berg, B. (2001). *Qualitative research methods for the social sciences* (4th ed.). Needeham, MA: Allyn & Bacon.

Cochran-Smith, M., & Lytle, S. (2009). *Inquiry as stance: Practitioner research for the next generation.* New York, NY: Teachers College Press.

Devetak, I., Glažar, I. A., & Vogrinc, J. (2010). The role of qualitative research in science education. *Eurasia Journal of Mathematics, Science & Technology Education*, 6(1), 77–84.

Driscoll, D. L., & Perdue, S. W. (2012). Theory, lore, and more: An analysis of RAD research in *The Writing Center Journal*, 1980–2009. *The Writing Center Journal*, 3(22), 11–39.

Fojas, C., Guevarra, R. P., & Sharma, N. T. (Eds.). (2018). *Beyond ethnicity: New politics of race in Hawai'i.* Honolulu: University of Hawai'i Press.

Fujikane, C., & Okamura, J. (Eds.). (2008). *Asian settler colonialism: From local governance to the habits of everyday life in Hawai'i.* Honolulu: University of Hawai'i Press.

Geertz, C. (1973). *The interpretation of cultures.* New York, NY: Basic Books.

Gillespie, P., Gillam, A., Brown, L. F., & Stay, B. (Eds.). (2002). *Writing center research: Extending the conversation*. Mahwah, NJ: Lawrence Erlbaum Associates.

Glaser, B. G., & Strauss, A. L. (1967). *The discovery of grounded theory: Strategies for qualitative research*. Chicago, IL: Aldine Publishing.

Harding, S. (1987). Introduction: Is there a feminist method? In S. Harding (Ed.), *Feminism and methodology: Social science issues* (pp. 1–14). Bloomington: Indiana University Press.

Haswell, R. H. (2005). NCTE/CCCC's recent war on scholarship. *Written Communication, 22*(2), 198–223.

Liggett, S., Jordan, K., & Price, S. (2011). Mapping knowledge-making in writing center research: A taxonomy of methodologies. *Writing Center Journal, 31*(2), 50–88.

Lunsford, A. (1992). Collaboration, control, and the idea of a writing center. *The Writing Center Journal, 12*(1), 3–10.

Miles, M. B., & Huberman, A. M. (1984). *Qualitative data analysis*. Beverly Hills, CA: Sage Publications.

North, S. M. (1 984). Writing center research: Testing our assumptions. In G.A. Olson (Ed.), *Writing centers: Theory and administration* (pp. 24–35). Urbana, IL: NCTE.

Rohrer, J. (2016). *Staking claim: Settler colonialism and racialization in Hawai'i*. Tucson: University of Arizona Press.

Smith, L. T. (1999). *Decolonizing methodologies: Research and indigenous peoples*. New York, NY: Zed Books.

3 A Practitioner's Inquiry into Tutor Professionalization *vis-à-vis* Collaboration

This chapter tells a story. I know I am not supposed to say that because doing so invokes all the critiques that too much of writing center research only amounts to lore. But it does tell a story. It is about how I got my center up and running in a new location as new faculty/director guided by the tenets of Practitioner Inquiry. This chapter also does more. Using that same model, Practitioner Inquiry, it presents an empirical investigation to determine the efficacy of the practices implemented in terms of the impact they had on the consultants working in the center. It is both, a story and an empirical investigation. As practitioners, our work involves people, and people come with stories. I think when we try to remove people and their stories from our research, we are in danger of compromising the very values at the heart of our work, values that remind us that we do this work because we value people and their stories. As writing center practitioners, we spend our careers listening to those stories so we can meet people where they are with supports that attend to their specific contingencies. I advocate Practitioner Inquiry precisely because it is a research model that centers the practitioner and the people they work with. The model does not allow a researcher to downplay their role or their impact on the process or the outcomes—indeed, they are foregrounded. So, the story that follows is about me and the consultants I work with in my center—but the empirical investigation into that work provides a template for others interested in examining the same or similar practices in their centers. The findings of the investigation point to a need to do so—or, at least, suggest a need to consider modulating claims about our work until we have research to support them.

This story and study engage two prominent claims: that our centers are collaborative, and that our consultants gain valuable skills through their work. Neither of these claims originated with me, but I have adopted them and work to ensure our center lives up to them.

Increasing attention on writing centers as pedagogical spaces that support consultant learning and professionalization has laid a foundation for inquiry into exactly what consultants gain from working in centers. Harvey Kail, Paula Gillespie, & Bradley Hughes's (2020) groundbreaking online project, *The Peer Writing Tutor Alumni Research Project*, is dedicated to examining what students get out of their "education and experience as peer writing tutors." One of the pages at the site, "Publications about Tutor Alumni Research and Tutor Learning," identifies 56 publications that, in different ways, address consultant learning. While a majority of these articles focus on skills consultants gain through the actual act of tutoring, several begin to explore the different skills consultants acquire through engagement in administration. Working together in administration draws attention to the director-consultant dynamic, yet little, if any, writing center scholarship or research has examined this relationship. Considering the centrality of collaboration in writing center pedagogy, inquiry into how collaboration is realized between the director and consultants specifically in the context of administration, and in what ways those collaborative efforts affect professionalization, seems an undertaking that could provide interesting insights.

In this chapter I discuss how I applied a Practitioner Inquiry methodology to the director-consultant work relationship to foster collaboration in the management of our center, and at the same time, used Practitioner Inquiry as a framework in an empirical investigation into the efficacy of this approach. This study details the collaborative approaches and practices implemented over the course of one academic year in the administration of our center. In terms of benefits realized by consultants, the focus encompasses center management and consultant training, but not necessarily actual consultant-writer interactions (although arguably it is impossible to separate these). I will discuss the ways emphasizing the consultants' knowledge and experiences in the creation of a shared vision for our center fostered collaboration and ownership of the center. To determine the effectiveness of this approach in terms of consultant learning and their professionalization, I conduct content analysis on consultants' end-of-semester anonymous evaluations of their experiences working in the center. With this study, I hope to move beyond a focus on collaboration in the consultant-writer relationship and demonstrate that implementing practices that enhance collaboration in the director-consultant relationship yields positive, practical results that add depth to our understandings of writing centers as collaborative and pedagogical spaces that support consultant learning and professionalization.

Understanding Centers as a Pedagogical Space for Consultants

While writing center literature examining consultant learning makes up a relatively small portion of writing center scholarship overall, there has been sustained attention to this important topic since the 1970s. The list of works included in "Publications about Tutor Alumni Research and Tutor Learning" (Kail, Gillespie, & Hughes, 2020) consists of 56 publications since 1978 and provides a comprehensive representation of the scholarship and research that has contributed to our understanding of what consultants gain from their work.[1] Moreover, looking at publication dates points to increasing interest in this area of research: among the 56 publications listed, 36 (63%) were published since 2000, and 25 of those 36 (69%) were published since 2005: eight in the *Writing Lab Newsletter* (*WLN*), three in *The Writing Center Journal* (*WCJ*), one in *Praxis: A Writing Center Journal* (*Praxis*), eight in anthologies or books, two in journals not specific to writing center studies, one in a conference proceeding, one is a dissertation, and one is a website. To better understand how consultant learning is being treated in writing center studies, I focus on 12 articles published since 2005 (one not included on Kail, Gillespie, & Hughes's (2020) list) in the three journals specifically focused on writing center studies: the *WLN*, *WCJ*, and *Praxis*.

Among the eight articles that have been published in *WLN*, three focus on what consultants gain from actual tutoring (Kedia, 2007; Monroe, 2007; Dinitz & Kiedaisch, 2009), three look specifically at the transferability of skills acquired as consultants for future teachers or in other jobs (Whalen, 2005; Hammerbacher, Phillips, & Tucker, 2006; Gerald, 2009), and one examines teachers who work in centers (Moneyhun & Hanlon-Baker, 2012).

While several of these articles mention administrative roles, only one of the eight *WLN* articles focuses solely on learning and skills acquired from such work. In "Shaping Careers in the Writing Center," Kathleen Welsch (2008) "examine[s] how writing centers contribute to the professional learning experience of our student staff," focusing on five areas: administration, public relations, client relations, writing, and personal professional development (p. 2). Welsch discusses the creation of administrative, public relations, and client relations "jobs" in her center that were filled by consultants and provides brief anecdotes from graduate assistants who worked in these positions and who attest to the positive experience and skill sets gained. In light of the positive outcomes Welsch and her team experienced, the article ends with Welsch advocating center practitioners to explore such options in their own centers.

The three articles in *WCJ* that address consultant learning examine different aspects of tutoring and the transfer of skills: Bradley Hughes, Paula Gillespie, & Harvey Kail (2010) provide an overview of the skills 126 former consultants indicated their working as peer consultants facilitated; Emily Isaacs & Ellen Kolba (2009) discuss pre-service teachers working in high school centers; and Kenneth Bruffee (2008) notes important skills gained from consultants teaching other consultants and briefly mentions administrative skills among these.

In Naomi Silver et al.'s (2009) *Praxis* article, "From Peer Tutors to Writing Center Colleagues," the authors discuss the implementation of a summer internship made available to two consultants and how the increased responsibilities in terms of training and center oversight provided an opportunity for "tutors to move beyond self-interest and gain a more holistic perspective on professional work." And, while not specifically addressing consultant learning (and not on Kail, Gillespie, & Hughes's list), Kelly Prajean's (2010) article "Reaching in, Reaching Out: A Tale of Administration Experimentation and the Process of Administrative Inclusion," details the creation of several administrative positions in her center and how working with her consultants as a team enabled her to accomplish things they would not have had they adhered to a director-consultant paradigm wherein administrative work is solely/mostly the responsibility of the director.

Collectively, this body of scholarship points to the potential for consultant learning that working in writing centers facilitates; it represents our centers as pedagogical spaces that engender consultant learning and subsequently professionalization in addition to providing support for writers across our campuses. This chapter furthers this work through an empirical investigation of the less-examined subtopic of the director-consultant relationship in the context of the administration of the center. Moreover, it acts as a case study that illustrates the efficacy of Practitioner Inquiry as a methodology for both practice and research.

Methodology

Collaboration is one of, if not *the*, key term associated with writing center work, and as with most writing center practitioners, it informs my work in multiple ways. I am interested in reinforcing collaboration as part of the tutoring environment in ways that move beyond the consultants' relationship with student-writers to include the director-consultant relationship. In this study, in addition to using Practitioner Inquiry to guide the empirical investigation, I employ Practitioner Inquiry in conjunction with the theory of collaboration I presented in Chapter 1 to guide my practice. As I will illustrate in the following sections, the model is well suited for fostering a multidirectional collaborative relationship between me, the teacher-director, and the student-consultants in an instructional setting in ways that can increase all participants' agency and professionalize the consultants at the same time.

Building on the literature reviewed earlier, this study attends to the need to further document the ways consultants benefit from their work in writing centers—this would be what John Creswell (2009) identifies as the research problem. My "central research question" (Creswell, 2009) needed to ground this broad topic so that concepts could be operationalized. I wanted to consider the intersection of several variables to address the research problem, namely, collaboration and professionalization, to better capture whether/how a collaborative environment facilitated professionalization. Determining if the environment is collaborative would be the obvious first step. Applying one of the tenets for collaboration as laid out in Chapter 2, in a collaborative environment, consultants should have input in and benefit from their work in our center in ways that are equitable with my input and benefit. By employing collaboration this way, in addition to informing how we, the consultants and I, work together in our center, it also positioned collaboration as a defining term to identify and assess benefits realized by all parties.

The other key concept examined in this project is consultant professionalization. In defining professionalization, I looked to general career-advice sources, as consultants may pursue a variety of jobs both within and outside academia. Consistent in several definitions of professionalism is the emphasis on attainment of "specialized knowledge" (Mindtools, 2019) or "competence" (Joseph, 2018). No matter how it is categorized, discussions of professionalization point to a commitment to, or investment in, developing and improving expertise to enhance job performance and improve the work environment. Professionalization thus has implications for confidence (confidence is specifically mentioned in both sources cited here)—particularly in the way attainment of specialized knowledge can facilitate an individual claiming agency over that knowledge in achievement of the goals (i.e., services provided) of a particular workplace. So, to demonstrate professionalization, in the data I would be looking for evidence of investment, confidence/agency, and specific learning outcomes *vis-à-vis* the work consultants perform in the center.

This project, however, is specifically designed to explore any intersection between collaboration and professionalization. Therefore, any benefits realized from a collaborative work environment would need to align with the attributes associated with professionalization. Foregrounding the conceptual frameworks outlined earlier, I designed the following two central research questions:

1. Was a collaborative environment achieved in the writing center, as evidenced by consultants, indicating they experienced (a) investment in the work and work environment, (b) agency in interactions and the work of the center, and (c) learning/acquisition of skills?
2. Did employing a collaborative approach to our work have a positive impact on consultants' professionalization?

Following the work of Matthew Miles & Michael Huberman (1994) on qualitative research methodologies, Creswell (2009) notes the need to articulate sub-questions that "narrow the focus of the study but leave open the questioning" (pp. 129–130). I thus identified two sets of sub-questions, one to inform each practice and research. When doing this, I remained particularly focused on how I was using collaboration as a frame to determine what all participants, the consultants and myself, brought to and gained from our work and the equity between the same. The first set of five sub-questions were designed for inquiry into collaboration in our praxis:

1. What sources of knowledge do the consultants bring?
2. How am I benefiting from the work consultants do?
3. How are the consultants benefiting?
4. What is the benefit to the center and those who use it?
5. Are the benefits fairly equitable or are they skewed to favor one party?

I then articulated four additional sub-questions to guide the research and provide a means to capture consultants' professionalization, from their perspective, *vis-à-vis* the collaborative framework described earlier:

1. Do the consultants experience the writing center as a collaborative space?
2. Do the consultants indicate they have agency in the running of the center?

3   Do the consultants indicate they are learning skills?
4   Overall, do the findings suggest a correlation between a collaborative work environment and professionalization?

Thus, in this study, Practitioner Inquiry is employed as a framework for praxis to foster a multidirectional collaborative relationship between the teacher-director and the student-consultants to increase consultants' agency. At the same time, Practitioner Inquiry informs the research design, particularly the goal of producing empirical research to document the efficacy of the approaches implemented in terms of professionalization by foregrounding the approaches laid out in Chapter 2: data triangulation, systematicity, and recursivity in data collection, analysis, and presentation.

In the next section, I discuss the approaches and practices implemented and articulate them with the first set of five sub-questions designed to guide approaches to praxis, highlighting the ways Practitioner Inquiry informed my approach. I incorporate qualitative excerpts from the responses to end-of-semester evaluations in this discussion to give a general sense of student responses to these practices. I will then follow with a quantitative treatment of the data gathered from the end-of-semester evaluations.

Collaboration as Professionalization: Interventions

To better capture the approaches initiated to facilitate collaboration as defined in the previous section by the first set of sub-questions, I offer here a brief explanation of the practices I implemented as director of our writing center. Throughout the discussion, I will add in parenthesis Q1, Q2, and so forth to refer to the specific sub-question a particular approach or practice addresses. During the period data were collected for this study, seven graduate assistants were assigned to the center in each semester: five from English and two from Second Language Studies. Undergraduate consultants are either simultaneously enrolled in a senior-level "Teaching Composition" course and, as part of the course practicum, work five hours per week as paid consultants, or have completed the course and been invited to continue as consultants. I refer to consultants who have worked in the center for more than one semester as "experienced," and those concurrently enrolled in the course as "new."

My first "job" as writing center director was to physically bring our center back to the English Department from the Learning Assistance Center, where it had been relocated several years prior. The move provided the perfect opportunity for a fresh start. I began envisioning ours as a "center for writers" rather than a writing center. Following others' examples, I wanted to expand the center in terms of services offered and create a space where writers could come even if they were not working with a consultant, where they could book tables for a writing group or just drop in to talk with other writers. Scholarship and Listserv discussions both indicate that writing centers, in general, are "active in being resource centers for teachers and students" (Harris qtd. in Threadgill, 2010, p. 20). Rebecca Jackson & Jackie Grutsch McKinney (2012) capture the growth in writing center services through a survey of over 141 centers with various institutional affiliations. Jackson & McKinney's survey indicates a veritable cornucopia of services that go beyond tutoring,[2] including room rental (23%), handouts (89%), writing groups (13.5%), dissertation/thesis writing groups (10%), and workshops for students (84%), faculty (59%), and staff (29%) (pp. 5–9).

The initiatives highlighted here are a just a sampling of the kinds of innovations and initiatives being explored at different centers and provided me with many examples that could be adapted to fulfill the needs of our center. When entertaining the possibilities, it was apparent to me that my position as faculty and director distanced me in certain ways from the student body such initiatives are meant to serve. I knew I could greatly benefit from the experiences and knowledge my staff brought as both consultants and students. I wanted to articulate an approach for working with the consultants that reinforced their investment in the center and facilitated a collaborative work relationship between all of us. I believe strongly that a work environment built on these premises would nurture the invaluable resource that is our consultants.

But at this point I was still working alone. To prepare the new writing center space, I, like so many other writing center practitioners, attended to the physical nature of the center: I cleaned and brought in a couch, tables, chairs, and plants; set up a coffee and tea station; put up wall hangings; joined the Listserv; subscribed to (inexpensive) appointment software (not really knowing what I needed); and set up weekly staff meetings and implemented a training plan that included readings, presentations, and time for consultants to share. The goal was to create a place where students felt welcome to hang out, working under the assumption that if students were "in" a space that was positively associated with writing, it could translate into positive relationships with writing. Every modification was intended to engender a collaborative, supportive space, but so much of this work took place prior to my actually meeting any consultants.

I attempted to counter my autonomy over these decisions by actively seeking the consultants' advice on the physical space, training, and session protocols once the semester began. The experienced consultants were quick to offer suggestions and provide input, and after the semester started, all changes, no matter how seemingly trivial, were discussed as a group. Maintaining transparency in terms of information proved to be key in establishing a collaborative environment. These efforts are informed by my practitioner "stance" (as explained in Chapter 1) and set the tone for our interactions, as is evidenced in one consultant's comment in the end-of semester evaluations: "[The Director] always discussed with us matters of importance (regarding policy and related updates) and went out of her way to instill a sense of agency and authority in us."[3]

Knowing there was more work than I could possibly do alone, I recruited my first Assistant Director. This student had worked as a consultant longer than any of the others and thus brought a lot of experience and knowledge to this new position (Q1). Creating this administrative position that drew on the consultant's knowledge reflects the Practitioner Inquiry position that values the knowledge others bring and assumes "those who work in a particular educational context ... have significant knowledge about those situations" (Cochran-Smith & Lytle, 2009, p. 42). The Assistant Director not only had lengthy tutoring experience, but was also a student at our institution, and, as such, possessed an understanding of the student body that differed from my own (Q1). We collaboratively agreed on the parameters of the job so that it met both of our needs and expectations. In terms of benefits, they would be graduating at the end of the semester and an administrative position would be a nice addition to their CV, so the benefits to both of us were material and immediate (Q2, Q3, and Q5).[4] The addition of this position became a significant step in characterizing our consultants as both experts and professionals, who have the skills and maturity—both academic and professional—to take on administrative roles and responsibilities in the center.

Cognizant of their workload, I maintained a heightened vigilance concerning benefits to me outweighing benefits to the consultants (Q5). As I actively explored ways to expand opportunities for the consultants to have input in administration so that they could gain transferable skills and experience, I was cautious of exploiting them. Focused on the foundational concepts aligned with Practitioner Inquiry, namely, collaboration and the social construction of knowledge, I proceeded informed by Marilyn Cochran-Smith & Susan Lytle's (1999) "ways of knowing in communities" because of its advocacy for "the conjoined efforts of teachers and students as inquirers [as a means to alter] the relations of power in the schools and universities" (p. 18). This pedagogical stance aligns with Andrea Lunsford's (1992) "idea of a writing center informed by a theory of knowledge as socially constructed ... that presents a challenge to the institution of higher education" (p. 5). With its emphasis on student empowerment, incorporating the social construction of knowledge into my stance in this way helped ensure I was not exploiting my consultants' desire to perform well in their jobs when presented with additional roles. This was, and still is, a tricky negotiation. The only way to really know if someone is feeling "pushed in a direction" rather than "offered welcome opportunities" is if they feel comfortable declining. I frequently asked the consultants in groups and individually if they had any concerns or felt overworked; however, I knew this did not entirely ensure candid responses. The end-of-semester evaluations thus became an important temperature check as did all eligible consultants requesting to continue to work in the center over the subsequent two semesters.

I continually tried to identify ways to add to my administrative support that created opportunities for the consultants to claim agency in the space. The consultants worked on mini-projects—such as updating our information flyer and the website, redefining our mission statement, and articulating learning outcomes for both writers who visit the center and consultants who work there—while I provided oversight. I was very careful not to undo or redo anyone's work; changes were discussed and negotiated, with the assumption that everyone brought expertise and knowledge to the conversation (Q1). I found that working with my consultants from this collaborative stance correlated to the consultants increasingly recognizing areas wherein they felt comfortable claiming agency. One student wrote in the end-of-semester evaluation, "[The Director] allows her employees room to grow and make decisions." And, another commented:

> I was pretty darn satisfied with the amount of trust [the Director] had in all of us, which translated to a healthy amount of autonomy and independence she afforded her staff. Though she was always clear and forthright about her expectations, [she] invariably treated us as emerging professionals capable of handling things well enough on our own.

If, as this statement suggests, the consultants were benefiting through academic maturation, both the center and I were also (Q2, Q3, and Q4). The center was bustling with activity from nine to five every day.

Indeed, that first year, we facilitated almost 2,000 appointments with students representing 123 different disciplines across campus. My colleagues often commented on the positive impact of the center, and, as a pre-tenured faculty, having this work recognized was a great benefit to me professionally (Q2).

In line with understanding our center as a pedagogical space that provides the consultants with a foundation in composition and writing center pedagogy (and now administration) (Q3), I next wanted to explore ways the experienced consultants could support the new consultants to add to their pedagogical experiences. Therefore, when it came time to incorporate the new consultants into the schedule, I turned to my experienced consultants for help with the orientation process. They are, after all, a significant source of knowledge when it comes to the everyday running of the center; in addition, some of them have worked in management and/or have extensive experience with training (Q1). Another key concern of mine was establishing a sense of camaraderie among all the consultants, similar to what had been established among the experienced consultants and myself.

I handed over the hours of availability of the new consultant to the Assistant Director and had him work with a fellow consultant to set up their schedules. We assigned each new consultant an experienced consultant "liaison" as their point of contact (Q1). Not only did this help me tremendously in the work of initiating the new consultants into the center (Q2), it worked to build a staff that became incredibly close and protective of each other. One consultant wrote on an evaluation, "Aside from the pleasure of talking to students about their writing, I really like the camaraderie the consultants had with each other." In the weekly meetings, which only graduate student and continuing experienced consultants attended, it was refreshing to hear how quickly the experienced consultants got to "know" the new consultants—they knew if they were having difficulties and frequently commented on tutoring styles. It became apparent to me that the experienced consultants were observing the new consultants, reflecting on their practices and learning from them (Q3). I began to see our center as a multidirectional learning environment. It is well-documented that consultants acquire a tremendous skill set from tutoring, but consultants in this case were learning not only from working with and observing other consultants but also, as Bruffee (2008) points out, from teaching other consultants.

With this basic foundation for working together in place, we decided to pursue some of our other goals for the center, being mindful of current scholarship on the robust range of services offered at other centers (Threadgill, 2010; Jackson & McKinney, 2012). When entertaining ideas for such services, my first concern was offering support to beginning college students, particularly those enrolled in First Year Writing (FYW). I raised the idea of creating workshops that the consultants could administer. I introduced the idea saying something like: "I have no idea what such a workshop can or should look like, I have no preconceived notions, I am open to all suggestions, who wants to take the project on?" Several of the consultants immediately expressed interest. What transpired next was nothing short of amazing, not just in terms of the workshops produced but also in terms of the ways these consultants engaged in this activity. What I observed as my consultants tackled this project suggests that having autonomy over a project fosters investment and adds another layer of skills to what consultants already learn from the more traditional aspects of the job, and through this work, they were defining their jobs themselves (Q3). The consultants had to report each week on progress to the whole group. Several of the consultants had a unique knowledge base to draw from as they had been or were currently course-embedded peer mentors in FYW courses. Whereas I work with peer mentors when I teach FYW, many of them had worked with several teachers, and thus brought a wide array of ideas on how to best serve the widest group of students (Q1).

Providing opportunities for the consultants to use their knowledge and implement ideas that they felt would help other students aligned with the basic principles of collaboration and social construction of knowledge for working within a Practitioner Inquiry frame—and the two proved intricately related. Articulating a collaborative framework for both the director-consultant and consultant-writer relationships engendered knowledge-building on multiple levels. The consultants were drawing from their experiences working in the center and synthesizing that with their experiences as mentors in FYW courses, all of which was fostered by continual discussion of scholarship. These new roles that drew from their work as consultants and mentors and included leadership activities engendered professionalization in different ways than only tutoring did. Two of the consultants took the lead on the workshop project: they scaffolded the project into discreet tasks and asked each member of our group to work on one item. In addition to building a workshop template, they organized meetings, incorporated everyone's ideas, and accomplished this work in a way that, remarkably, increased the aura of collaboration in the center. In the evaluations, one consultant suggested that the workshop projects "[made] us feel like we all played an important part in a successful center," and another stated, "I am certain that all consultants felt that we were contributing."

I was inspired by what I watched evolve in the consultants over the semester—as a team and individuals, they simply exceeded my expectations in every aspect of their jobs. By the end of that first year, there were two titled positions: Assistant Director and Workshop Coordinator. Assigning titles may seem a small thing, but, according to my staff, it changed the way they understand their roles in the center. One consultant commented:

> I must admit that when I was assigned the title of Workshop Coordinator, it helped me to understand the responsibilities that I had been given. I forced myself to take a more involved approach to being an administrator, and taking an active role in delegating responsibilities and effectively supporting the other consultants in their assignments.

The titled positions, that at the time had no clear job descriptions, somehow pushed the students to perform in ways they had not previously. One consultant related,

> I can say with confidence that the assigning of titles along with additional duties only enhanced our prospects as emerging professionals... These duties required skills and habits that will serve me quite well in both academic and non-academic professional settings.

Triangulation: Quantitative Data

In the previous section, I include several excerpts from the end-of-semester consultant evaluations; however, selecting particular qualitative data to demonstrate positive response to a particular approach allows for a certain bias in the representation of data. To counter this bias, I triangulate these excerpts with a qualitative and quantitative analysis of the same evaluation responses. These data consist of answers to two end-of-semester writing center evaluations (fall and spring) made up of four questions written and administered by the Assistant Director. The following questions were designed prior to the inception of this project, and not for the specific purpose of collecting data to address the previously noted research questions:

1   Reflecting upon the writing center meetings you participated in, the supervision you received, and your overall work experience in the center this semester, please identify and discuss the areas you were satisfied with.

88 *Practitioner's Inquiry*

2   Please identify and discuss the areas you would change (in other words, improve, eliminate, etc.), and, if possible, how you would change them.
3   Please identify and discuss areas, topics, or issues that you wish were addressed or addressed more during the meetings.
4   Please provide any additional comments about the training and supervision you received from [the director] this semester.

For this project, seven experienced consultants are the "participants" from whom data were gathered to evaluate the approach documented here. I focus on these consultants because they all worked in the center for an entire year; worked twice as many hours weekly as new consultants; and as the new consultants were simultaneously enrolled in the corresponding practicum course for at least one of the semesters, they filled out a different end-of-semester evaluation in adherence to departmental protocol.

For the fall semester, all seven consultants responded to the evaluation; however, inconsistently across questions: seven consultants responded to questions one and two, and six consultants responded to questions three and four. In the spring semester, again all seven consultants responded to the evaluation, but, also again, inconsistently: seven consultants responded to questions one and four, and six consultants responded to questions two and three. Table 3.1 reflects a breakdown of responses for the two semesters. Across both semesters, there were a total of 52 responses in 14 evaluations. All responses were included as data.

I approached analysis of the data in two ways, both which involve content analysis at the word level, which Bruce Berg (2001) explains as "the smallest element or unit used in content analysis. Its use generally results in a frequency distribution of specified words or terms" (p. 246). To capture the frequency to which collaboration, agency, learning, and investment were realized in terms of practice and

Table 3.1 Summary of Number of Evaluation Responses for Each Question

Evaluation Question	Fall # of Responses	Spring # of Responses	Total # of Responses
Question 1	7	7	14
Question 2	7	6	13
Question 3	6	6	12
Question 4	6	7	13
Total responses	26	26	52

benefits: (1) I conducted qualitative analysis by in vivo coding the written responses for themes, and (2) to triangulate these findings, I quantified usage of collective pronouns—we, us, our—and examined their use in terms inclusivity/exclusivity.

Following both Creswell's (2009) and Johnny Saldaña's (2009) recommended processes, I first read though all 52 responses to get a general sense of the information, highlighting sentences or phrases that caught my attention in the context of the study. I then created a table with the sentences or clauses and went through them to identify in vivo codes—codes taken directly from what a participant wrote. I employed an "Affective Coding Method," as this method "investigate[s] subjective qualities of human experience (e.g., emotions, values, conflicts, judgments) by directly acknowledging and naming those experiences" (Saldaña, 2009, p. 86), which seemed the method most appropriate to uncover consultant's perceptions about and reactions to their work. I then condensed codes into words. Except where meaning was obviously deviant, all forms of a word encompassed one code; for example, independent, independence, independently were grouped together within the code "independent." I practiced recursivity throughout, sometimes recoding and recategorizing as I pondered different implications of written responses, codes, and categories.

Table 3.2 lists the in vivo codes that were grouped together, the corresponding number of times a code appeared, and the category that was created for the grouping. When grouping, I looked for codes that addressed my original research questions and the sub-questions, specifically investment, confidence/agency, skills acquisition/learning, and, the important overarching variable, collaboration. It is important to note that when considering the number of times a listed word appeared, only instances that aligned with actual consultant experience were counted. For example, "Open" was counted when referring to "open discussion," "open for feedback," but not for "open the center earlier." Since I had decided to use in vivo coding, if a meaning was vague or unclear, I left it out of my count.

The naming of the categories for Groups 1 and 2 was rather straightforward: the cluster of codes in Group 1 represents behaviors and experiences that suggest consultants having Agency. For Group 2, the words all point to consultants being supported in some way, so I named the category Support. (Important to note here as it relates to the discussion of inclusive and exclusive *we* that follows is that the agent doing the support is me, the director; so, the director encouraged, nurtured, supported the consultants). Group 3 became the category Investment. The codes included in this group were taken from

Table 3.2 In Vivo Groupings

Group 1: CAT: Agency	#	Group 2: CAT: Support	#	Group 3: CAT: Investment	#	Group 4: CAT: Collaboration	#	Group 5: CAT: Learning	#
Code		Code		Code		Code		Code	
Agency	1	Support	5	Would (do…)	10	Tutors and Director	3	Useful	3
Authority	1	Nurture	1	Should (do…)	2	Camaraderie	1	Learn	7
Independence	3	Provided us	2	Could (do…)	1	Open	2	Become	1
Grow	1	Gave us	2	Expect (to do…)	1	Team	1	Develop	1
Make Decisions	1	Received	1						
Find our own way	1	Encouraged	5						
Trust	2	Addressed	4						
Contribute	1	Helped	10						
Confidence	5	Safe	3						
Totals	**16**		**33**		**14**		**7**		**12**

Practitioner's Inquiry 91

statements in which the consultants made explicit suggestions for training or administration, with 11 suggestions applicable to training and five to administration. The feature of professionalization operationalized for this study is "a commitment to, or investment in, developing and improving expertise to enhance job performance and improve the work environment" (see pp. 5–6). I posit that making suggestions for training and administration reflect investment in the workplace and a desire to improve job performance, both elements of professionalization as defined here. Group 4 was labeled Collaboration as this is a primary theme in this study, and these words/phrases suggest collaboration. Lastly, as part of the collaborative approach includes ensuring all participants benefit and because in the evaluations consultants specifically (and unsolicited) identified what they learned, Learning was identified as the last category.

The categories are all operationalized, either directly or indirectly, in the sub-questions informing this study:

1 Do the consultants experience the writing center as a collaborative space?
2 Do the consultants indicate they have agency in the running of the center?
3 Do the consultants indicate they are learning skills?
4 Overall, do the findings suggest a correlation between a collaborative work environment and professionalization?

Before addressing the categories with highest and lowest number of references, Support (33) and Collaboration (7), I will first discuss the three categories with relatively similar numbers of references (Agency 16; Investment, 14; Learning, 12) in relation to questions two, three, and four. Unsolicited by the questions, consultants consistently mentioned that they felt they could exercise agency in the space whether literally through decision-making or having a sense of growing confidence. That Agency was referenced, on average, more than once per each evaluation (14 total evaluations, seven each semester) suggests that consultants felt they did have agency to some extent. The evaluation questions similarly did not specifically ask about consultants' learning; however, almost all consultants addressed specific things they learned across both semesters. The overt acknowledgment that they were learning and acquiring skills contextualizes the center as a pedagogical space for consultants and indicates they realized a benefit to their work. This acquisition of skills also points to professional development in the context of how the term is defined here. In terms of the Investment category, to be fair, one of the evaluation questions specifically asks for consultant's suggestions, although the question did not give any direction for these suggestions. Overwhelmingly, consultants offered suggestions on training, and, to lesser degree, on administration. As such, these suggestions imply the consultants' investment in their own improvement through training that enables them to better do their jobs.

Overall, I believe the findings point to adequate evidence that consultants felt they had agency, showed a level of investment through articulation of ways to expand training, and that they were actively learning skills that enabled them to perform better—outcomes all aligned with professionalization. These characteristics are also used to evaluate "collaboration" as articulated in the first central research question, as there is indication a collaborative environment was achieved. Interestingly, however, collaboration was not alluded to as frequently in the evaluations. To further examine collaboration, I now turn to the Support and Collaboration categories.

Support had double the number of references compared to all other categories. I see this as a positive outcome. As the director, I should be providing support in terms of both soft (confidence, agency) and hard (specific tutoring strategies) skills. While achieving a collaborative environment is key for me, especially in that I believe a collaborative environment fosters consultants' professional development, as the director, I still need to provide the model and direction—at least until consultants acquire enough experience and grounding in the scholarship to claim more agency in their own development. Interestingly, direct references to collaboration were fewer than in any other category. The extent to which Support was referenced, and collaboration was not, has implications for understanding how collaboration was enacted in the center, a topic I explore in the following discussion of the collective pronoun *we* as inclusive and exclusive.

To more fully capture the extent to which collaboration was realized and to provide a data set to triangulate the findings discussed earlier, I conducted quantitative analysis of words and sentences and compared uses of the collective pronouns (*we, our, us*) to the singular *I*. Table 3.3 presents the number of times each pronoun was used and the ratio of plural pronoun usage to singular.

I further examined uses of *we* in light of linguistics research that complicates the use of *we* in terms of how it constructs collectivity. Joanne Scheibman (2014) notes, "First person non-singular expressions reveal ways in which speakers align themselves with other individuals and groups in discourse. These uses also draw attention to the types of collectivities participants routinely identify with in a

Table 3.3 Comparison of Singular to Collective Pronoun Usage

Semester	# of Times I Used	Total # of Times we Used ----- # of Times Exclusive we Used	# of Times us Used	# of Times our Used	Total # of Times Collective Pronouns Used	% of Collective Pronoun Usage (Denominator = Column 2 + Column 6)
Fall	36	18 ---- 12 (67%)	10	5	33	48%
Spring	32	10 ---- 7 (70%)	4	7	21	40%
Total	68	28 ---- 19 (68%)	14	12	54	44%

given language community" (p. 23). Specifically, research on *we* usage articulates "grammatical distinctions between the inclusive and exclusive" (p. 24). Inclusivity is frequently represented through present tense predicates or use of modals (can, could, may, might, must, ought to, shall, should, will, and would), and exclusivity through past tense predicates (24). The numerical data below the dotted line in the "# of times *we* is used" column in Table 3.3 represent the number of times and corresponding percentage *we* appeared with past tense predicates, which would suggest exclusivity.

After examining how *we* is used in the evaluations in light of the linguistic scholarship on *we*, I identified two uses of *we*: (1) an inclusive *we* referring to the consultants and me, the director; and (2) an exclusive *we* that refers to only the consultants, separate from me. The data indicate that overall plural pronoun usage is close to 44% compared to the number of times consultants invoked a singular *I* (56%), suggesting that the consultants do align with a group; however, examining *we* in terms of inclusivity and exclusivity complicates this finding. Consultants overwhelmingly employed an exclusive use of *we* (68%), suggesting that the *we* excluded the addressee (Scheibman, 2014, p. 24), which, in this case, would be me, the director.

These findings are particularly interesting in terms of applications and claims of collaboration in writing centers. In this particular case, the data suggest that efforts to facilitate a collaborative environment were realized, but not to the full extent intended. If the consultants' use of *we* is representative of their experience working in the center and an indication of the collectivity they align themselves most frequently with, then they often see me, the director, as apart from that group. This finding aligns with the earlier discussion of the Support category. I do not necessarily see this outcome as negative: I am the director after all, and I should be providing both support and training to the consultants. However, these findings do complicate claims of collaboration, in particular, the extent to which a collaborative environment was achieved between the director and the consultants. Moreover, that 30% of the time the inclusive *we* is used could point to a shift from consultants aligning themselves mostly with only other consultants to seeing all of us as one group. This finding in particular would be interesting to track over time as consultants work in a center longer to determine if the ratio shifts to favor the inclusive *we*.

Overall, in terms of the central research questions discussed, the data gathered from the open-ended evaluation questions indicate that a collaborative environment was achieved, although perhaps not in the way I expected. Consultants noted ways they benefited from their experience working in the center and, as indicated by their suggestions for training and policy, were invested in their work, both which also point to professionalization. The data do not draw an explicit connection between collaboration and professionalization, although a correlation is implied. The collaborative approach to running the center provided space for the consultants to claim agency, and this arguably led to their feeling comfortable enough to make suggestions for improvement. It does seem that the consultants see themselves as being a part of a distinct group separate from me. I think this is both productive and points to the ways practices can be shaped going forward to facilitate a next all-inclusive level of collaboration.

End-of-semester evaluations, such as the discussed here, are a valid form of data for assessing whether Practitioner Inquiry is a viable framework that supports both collaboration and research in the writing center; however, it is only one form of data, and in this case, has been used to evaluate only one year and one set of consultants. To determine the efficacy of the practices I discuss here in terms of professionalization, more data need to be collected and outcomes need to be documented over time. The next phase of this project would therefore require further operationalization of the term professionalization, specifically in terms of collaboration, continued documentation of consultant's evaluations of practices for at least one additional year, and the implementation of an assessment tool designed to gather feedback specific to the assignation of administrative roles in the center.

Conclusion: Next Steps

When we talk about collaboration in writing center pedagogy, much of the focus has been on the consultant-writer relationship. Yet, there is another relationship that has tremendous impact on any center: the director-consultant relationship. And, while consultant learning has gained traction in our professional conversations, how they learn through engagement with administrative work is less explored. My hope is that the research presented here addresses the increasing interest in what has been a relatively under-examined but potentially highly impactful outcome of writing center work—consultant learning *vis-à-vis* collaborating with the director in administrative tasks. After all, recasting our centers as not only providing a service that supports writers across our campuses, but as a pedagogical space that provides consultants with training and skills that benefit them in careers both in and out of academia, elevates the work we do in significant ways. This study illustrates that implementing practices that enhance collaboration in the director-consultant relationship adds depth to the collaborative nature of the center and ultimately has implications for consultant learning. In this study, Practitioner Inquiry informed practices that created space for us to incorporate the consultants' wide array of skills and knowledge, and also provided a model for assessing and theorizing these practices that align with both writing center and empirical research, making it an ideal framework for conducting research in the writing center.

Notes

1. I would like to acknowledge and thank Harvey Kail, Paula Gillespie, and Bradley Hughes for making this rich resource available.
2. The following numbers in parenthesis indicate the percentage of respondents offering the respective service.
3. Although I use gender neutral pronouns in this article, excerpts from student evaluations appear verbatim, and pronoun usage remains as originally written by the students.
4. Following their graduation, this consultant went on to secure a job as a writing center director.

References

Berg, B. (2001). *Qualitative research methods for the social sciences* (4th ed.). Needham Heights, MA: Allyn & Bacon.

Bruffee, K. A. (2008). What being a writing peer tutor can do for you. *The Writing Center Journal, 28*(2), 5–10.

Cochran-Smith, M., & Lytle, S. (1999). The teacher research movement: The next decade. *Educational Researcher, 28*(15), 15–25.

Cochran-Smith, M., & Lytle, S. (2009). *Inquiry as stance: Practitioner research for the next generation.* New York, NY: Teachers College Press.

Creswell, J. (2009). *Research design: Qualitative, quantitative, and mixed methods approaches.* Thousand Oaks, CA: Sage Publications.

Dinitz, S., & Kiedaisch, J. (2009). Tutoring writing as career development. *The Writing Lab Newsletter, 34*(3), 1–5.

Gerald, A. S. (2009). Back to the center: A former tutor reflects. *The Writing Lab Newsletter, 33*(8), 11–13.

Hammerbacher, M., Phillips, J., & Tucker, S. (2006). The road less traveled: English education majors applying practice and pedagogy. *The Writing Lab Newsletter, 30*(8), 14–16.

Hughes, B., Gillespie, P., & Kail, H. (2010). What they take with them: Findings from the peer writing tutor alumni research project. *The Writing Center Journal, 30*(2), 12–46.

Isaacs, E., & Kolba, E. (2009). Mutual benefits: Pre-service teachers and public-school students in the writing center. *The Writing Center Journal, 29*(2), 52–74.

Jackson, R., & McKinney, J. G. (2012). Beyond tutoring: Mapping the invisible landscape of writing center work. *Praxis: A Writing Center Journal, 9*(1), Retrieved January 20, 2019 from http://www.praxisuwc.com/jackson-mckinney-91.

Joseph, C. (2018). 10 Characteristics of professionalism. *Small business - Chron.com.* Retrieved February 10, 2019 from http://smallbusiness.chron.com/10-characteristics-professionalism-708.html.

Kail, H., Gillespie, P., & Hughes, B. (2020). *The peer writing tutor alumni research project.* Retrieved November 20, 2018 from http://www.writing.wisc.edu/pwtarp/.

Kedia, S. (2007). Everything I needed to know about life I learned at the writing center. *The Writing Lab Newsletter, 31*(7), 13–15.

Lunsford, A. (1992). Collaboration, control, and the idea of a writing center. *The Writing Center Journal, 12*(1), 3–10.

Miles, M. B., & Huberman, A. M. (1994). *Qualitative data analysis: A sourcebook of new methods.* Thousand Oaks, CA: Sage Publications.

Mindtools Content Team. (2019). Professionalism: Developing this vital characteristic. *Mindtools, Essential Skills for an Excellent Career.* Retrieved January 20, 2019 from https://www.mindtools.com/pages/article/professionalism.htm.

Moneyhun, C., & Hanlon-Baker, P. (2012). Tutoring teachers. *The Writing Lab Newsletter, 36*(9–10), 1–5.

Monroe, M. (2007). Reflection: How the writing center rekindled my passion and purpose to teach. *The Writing Lab Newsletter, 31*(6), 14–15.

Prajean, K. (2010). Reaching in, reaching out: A tale of administration experimentation and the process of administrative inclusion. *Praxis: A*

Writing Center Journal, 7(2). Retrieved November 19, 2018 from http://www.praxisuwc.com/prejean-72

Saldaña, J. (2009). *Coding manual for qualitative researchers*. Thousand Oaks, CA: Sage Publications.

Scheibman, J. (2014). Referentiality, predicate patterns, and functions of *we*-utterances in American English interactions. In T. Pavlidou (Ed.), *Constructing Collectivity: 'We' Across Languages and Contexts* (pp. 23–44). Amsterdam: John Benjamins Publishing.

Silver, N., Luke, C., Nieman, L., & Primo, N. (2009). From peer tutors to writing center colleagues. *Praxis: A Writing Center Journal*, 7(1). Retrieved November 10, 2018 from http://www.praxisuwc.com/silver-et-al-71.

Threadgill, E. (2010). Writing center work bridging boundaries: An interview with Muriel Harris. *Journal of Developmental Education*, 34(2), 20–22.

Welsch, K. (2008). Shaping careers in the writing center. *The Writing Lab Newsletter*, 32(8), 1–8.

Whalen, L. (2005). Putting your writing center experience to work. *The Writing Lab Newsletter*, 29(9), 9–10.

4 Translingual Practices vs. Academic Discourse

Writing Center Consultants Weigh in on Supporting Writers' Multiliteracy Repertoires

> Ethnic identity is twin skin to linguistic identity-I am my language. Until I can take pride in my language, I cannot take pride in myself.
> Gloria Anzaldua, Borderlands/La Frontera: The New Mestiza, 1987, p. 81

As I have noted in previous chapters, the location of our center at the University of Hawai'i at Mānoa (UHM) presents a distinct set of exigencies—as do the locations of all our places of practice. In Hawai'i, the impacts of colonization are tangible all around us, and many ongoing issues stemming from that colonization circulate around the politics of language use. The native language of Hawai'i, 'ōlelo Hawai'i, was banned as a medium of instruction in 1896 following the illegal overthrow of the Hawaiian kingdom, and it was not until 1978 that it was reinstated as one of the official languages of Hawai'i, the other being English. A Creole evolved in the Islands (Hawai'i Creole, or more commonly called Pidgin) and became a dominant language among Kanaka Maoli and the immigrant laborers brought to the islands to work the plantations and their descendants,[1] yet this language has also been disenfranchised. Despite its recognition as an official language of Hawai'i by the US Census in 2015, Pidgin is still an inferiority marker and its speakers are still often stigmatized.

My own journey with understanding language disenfranchisement is rooted in my upbringing. I grew up moving between Pidgin and "Standard English"[2]—often referred to as "proper English" by our elders and teachers—depending on where I was and who I was speaking with. I did not question why we were told not to speak Pidgin in the house or at school. On the Windward side of O'ahu, where I grew up, 'ōlelo Hawai'i was all around—on signs and woven into conversations that were predominantly conducted in English or Pidgin. But not in school. I just accepted these language dynamics—probably like so many other kids. But as I moved into adulthood, I began to question what it meant when people are told they cannot speak their language in certain contexts. I began to ask why 'ōlelo Hawai'i was not heard everywhere when it is the native language of this place. I left for Japan when I was 19, where I would live for ten years and become fluent in Japanese. That language experience raised even more questions for me. Speaking multiple languages was welcome and supported in Japan, with many people speaking another language in addition to Japanese. In contrast, in the United States, the dominance of English comes at the expense of other languages. Gloria Anzaldua's experiences depicted in "How to Tame A Wild Tongue," from which the quote that opens this chapter is taken, resonated with me. Anzaldua gave me words to understand the profound impact these experiences had on me and the ways I forged my own subjectivity. More importantly, it engendered an awareness of my own privilege in being able to speak and write "proper" English when the situation called for it or it suited my purpose. I know many people who do not have the same agility with this form of English, and I have heard more times than I care to recount some of these same people tell me in different ways that their English-language abilities limit their success, or worse, make them "not smart." What is even more heartbreaking is that I have witnessed these same values reproduced intergenerationally when Pidgin-speaking parents scold their children for speaking the language, reminding them if they do not speak "proper" English, they will not do good in school or ever get a good job.

These language dynamics are further complicated in our writing center, as each semester, approximately 50% of all visitors claim a language other than English as their primary language—but rarely is this language 'ōlelo Hawai'i or Pidgin. Many of our consultants speak more than one language, and we regularly have at least two consultants whose primary language is not English. As a center, we are invested in countering hegemonic structures that privilege certain ways of knowing, being, and communicating. We strive to support students so that they have space to claim agency over literacy repertoires that reflect and represent their lived experiences in specific geographically located communities. The politics of language use in Hawai'i influences our center's position *vis-à-vis* respecting and including multiple literacy practices in particular ways. For example, the students I work with have models for including different language resources in writing. As I do in my own writing, many scholars from Hawai'i, including most of the Kanaka Maoli scholars whose work I cite in the book, write Kanaka Maoli concepts in ʻōlelo Hawaiʻi when they refer to them, and it has become common practice not to italicize any words in ʻōlelo Hawaiʻi because they are not foreign in Hawaiʻi. While this practice is a significant political statement, it is a practice that works in this specific context to respond to the particular linguistic disenfranchisement that occurred here. Models for how to engage an analogous practice or to accommodate other ways of including multiple linguistic resources in published writing are not as readily available.

Against this backdrop, it is easy to understand that language issues are common topics of discussion in our center. One issue that we have continually revisited over the years—a question I am repeatedly asked by our consultants, and one I do not have a good answer for—goes something like this:

> Are we hypocrites when we claim to support diversity and inclusion—students' located and individual ways of knowing, being, and expressing themselves—but are also the medium through which the privileging of standard academic discourse is implicitly reproduced in our work with student writers because varied literacy constructions are ok as part of the process but not the product?

As we regularly revisit this question, conversations in our staff meetings have increasingly turned to scholarship on translanguaging and translingual approaches to supporting writing over the last decade, as they attend to practices of employing multiple linguistic codes that inform the literacy repertoires students draw from in meaning-making. But, as I will further explain in the next section, while promising, the scholarship falls short of providing a clear direction to respond to my consultants' question. When I had the opportunity to work at the National University of Ireland, Galway's (NUIG) Academic Writing Centre for a semester through the Fulbright Scholar Award Program, I was presented with the perfect opportunity to investigate how such issues are perceived and negotiated by writing center consultants in a different geographic location, Ireland. The long history of language suppression due to British colonization, and efforts at language revitalization that gained traction over the last century,[3] suggested similarities to my own practice site. It seemed an ideal situation to compare how two groups of college students living and working in very different geographic and sociopolitical contexts, yet with similar experiences of language colonization and revitalization, negotiate their work with writers with various literacy repertoires. This chapter presents the empirical qualitative study conducted in these two locations among the two cohorts of writing center consultants and its findings. But before moving to describing the study—which focuses on what writing center consultants say about these language issues, and how it affects their work with writers—I first turn to the scholarly conversations on translanguaging and translingual approaches to support writing, so that the two cohorts' responses, in addition to being compared with each other, can be situated in and against the scholarship.

The Scholarly Positions

While the language politics we negotiate in Hawai'i may not be universal, attention to issues surrounding language use in the scholarship over the last two decades indicates that practitioners in other places are concerned with acknowledging and supporting individuals' varied and multiple linguistic resources. Suresh Canagarajah, arguably one of the most prolific scholars on multilingual communication, helped to usher in the concept of *Translanguaging* in Composition Studies to capture the dynamics of negotiating multiple linguistic resources and literacy repertoires. Canagarajah (2011) explains translanguaging as representing the following set of "assumptions":

> for multilinguals, languages are part of a repertoire that is accessed for their communicative purposes; languages are not discrete and separated, but form an integrated system for them; multilingual competence emerges out of local practices where multiple languages are negotiated for communication; competence doesn't consist of separate competencies for each language, but a multicompetence that functions symbiotically for the different languages in one's repertoire; and, for these reasons, proficiency for multilinguals is focused on repertoire building – i.e., developing abilities in the different functions served by different languages – rather than total mastery over each and every language.
>
> (p. 1)

Collectively, the assumptions explain that individuals engage with multiple language resources fluidly as they weave various codes in the meaning-making process. And just like a tapestry, removing a thread changes the fabric in ways that are often damaging to the cloth's integrity. In Composition Studies, *code-meshing* and *translingual writing* are the terms most often used to describe the phenomenon of translanguaging, or making use of multiple linguistic codes and literacy repertoires in instances of communication in a single context (Canagarajah, 2011, p. 2). In addition to representing the act of using multiple codes, translingual is also used to articulate pedagogical approaches in efforts to support translingual students. But invariably, no matter which specific term is being employed, the scholarship points to these concepts as having social justice implications in their insistence on the democratization of language use.

When approaching language use as a social justice issue, translanguaging is appealing as it stands in direct opposition to the "commonly accepted" idea of code-switching. Code-switching has long been advocated in many locations, particularly schools, "where students are instructed to switch from one code or dialect to another...according to setting and audience" (Young et al., 2014, p. 2). For example, in Hawai'i, speaking Pidgin is fine (or mostly fine), as long as you can switch to Standard English at school, work, or when with people who do not speak Pidgin. The problems with code-switching are palpable when we understand language use as intricately tied to identity—suggesting a certain language is inappropriate for certain contexts correlates to the identity associated with that language use also being marginalized. Young et al. (2014) explain how this can play out in a school context:

> Given the central role of language variation in the expressions of individual identity, attempts to banish undervalued Englishes from the classroom place restrictions on students' ability to use the form of language that serve to convey emotions, attitudes, and relationships to other speakers. Because prescriptive language ideology generally treats undervalued varieties as "wrong" on the one hand or "inappropriate" in a certain context on the other, children who speak undervalued Englishes may feel as if school assumes they are "wrong" even when their answer is actually correct.
>
> (p. 33)

While Young et al. (2014) focus on the marginalization of English variations, these issues similarly impact speakers who negotiate languages other than English, as Anzaldua (1987) succinctly articulates: "Repeated attacks on our native tongue diminishes our sense of self" (p. 80). In the "Introduction: Code-Meshing as World Language," Young, Martinez, & Naviaux (2011) capture the political implications of code-switching when they describe it as emerging from "traditional English-only ideologies that require multilingual/multidialectal students to choose one code over another while privileging codes associated with dominant races and further alienating the codes of traditionally oppressed peoples" (p. xxiv). Such a paradigm for language use—privileging one language over all others—is reductive in its ability to reflect ways of knowing and being in the world not readily representable in dominant American literacy practices. It assumes nothing is lost when trying to capture experiences, ideas, or relationships represented by a single word in another language for which there is no comparison in English.[4]

In contrast, translanguaging (or code-meshing) allows for a linguistic complexity and multiplicity so that a wider range of experiences can be better depicted. Returning to Anzaldua's work, the many phrases in variations of her "home" languages that intersperse the mostly English text in "How to Tame a Wild Tongue" do much more than provide alternative meanings to what would have been enabled by a translation into English; the meshing of codes also captures how the languages interact for a multilingual to form their worldview. This interweaving also presents challenges for monolingual English readers as it can put an English-only reader in the multilingual writer's position of having to negotiate multiple and sometimes conflicting codes. Considering the increased awareness of the multiple linguistic resources students in our institutions bring with them,[5] it is absolutely a social justice issue to create space for them to represent their ideas and experiences using literacy repertoires that they feel best capture their lived realities. Indeed, Young, Martinez, & Naviaux (2011) describe code-meshing as a "right," arguing students should be able

> to blend accents, dialects, and varieties of English with school-based, academic, professional, and public Englishes, in any and all formal and informal contexts. English speakers' right to code-mesh includes the use of home languages, dialects, and accents beyond conversations with friends and family.
>
> (p. xxi)

The authors go on to proclaim that such a practice "promotes linguistic democracy" (p. xxiv). Indisputably, the more varied the linguistic codes a speaker or writer uses, the more work it will entail for some to comprehend. While I personally believe speaking and writing that incorporates this kind of variety adds a richness and engenders a deeper understanding of other worldviews, it undoubtedly presents challenges our current educational contexts are not yet prepared to deal with.

In an effort to promote translanguaging as an attribute, resource, and a right, rather than a deficit, scholars have articulated pedagogical approaches to support students who translanguage in their academic performances, whether speaking or writing. Bruce Horner et al. (2011) authored "Language Difference in Writing: Toward a Translingual Approach," a manifesto which advocates a translingual approach that "sees difference in language not as a barrier to overcome or a problem to manage, but as a resource for producing meaning in writing, speaking, reading, and listening" (p. 303). The 2016 Special Issue of *College English*, *Translingual Work in Composition* "reflects and builds on the efforts prompted" by Horner et al.'s earlier work by critically engaging with both the potential and caveats presented by translingual approaches. The editors, Min Zhan Lu & Bruce Horner (2016), highlighting its democratizing potential, position translingual approaches as the "other" in relation to "what monolingualist ideology would have us understand normal language use, users, and relations to be" (p. 212). But as critical engagement should, the Special Issue also features cautionary takes. Keith Gilyard (2016) counsels against embracing all language difference as the same, arguing it can work to flatten difference and mask the history of disenfranchisement experienced by marginalized language speakers:

> A possible consequence of positing a sameness of difference [across all kinds of translingualism] is that needed academic allies could read such a maneuver as a devaluing of the historical and unresolved struggles of groups that have been traditionally underrepresented in the academy and suffer disproportionately in relation to it.
>
> (p. 286)

Gilyard's position is similar to that of Scott Richard Lyons's (2009), who argues that hybrid language approaches and code-meshing can compromise sovereignty and language revitalization efforts for Native peoples. Both Gilyard and Lyons point to problems of wholesale adoption of any approach, the need to address exigencies of specific language communities, and the necessity of being guided by language stewards when considering the appropriateness of translingual approaches in any context.

Supporting students and their multiple linguistic repertoires has also long been at issue in writing center studies. And, similar to the trajectory in Composition Studies in general, the literature has moved from solely working to facilitate student writers' acquisition of errorless Standard English, to efforts at acknowledging varied literacy strategies. Thirty years ago, Anne DiPardo's (1992) acclaimed essay "'Whispers of coming and going': Lessons from Fannie," provided insights into "the social and linguistic challenges which inform [non-Anglo students'] struggles" (p. 125). In the ensuing decades, writing center scholarship has regularly featured pedagogical approaches for working with multilingual students, with the focus increasingly on strategies that affirm multiple identities, linguistic practices, and literacy repertoires. In their most recent issue, *The Writing Center Journal* editors (2019) describe this movement as a "collective call, across writing center and composition worlds, to foreground historically marginalized voices and to work more assertively to bridge divides, despite the discomfort often accompanying such work" (Bromley, Northway, & Schonberg, 2019, p. 12). Translingual approaches is one project answering this call. But, as the scholarship points out, there are numerous challenges such an approach presents—not the least of which is that what may be deemed appropriate translanguaging in our courses or in our centers may require significant mediation when negotiating expectations in other courses and in other disciplines.

The consultants I work/ed with at both UHM and NUIG are familiar with these trends in the scholarship, and they are well trained at adapting advocated strategies. As they are a primary support for writers in our institutions, they are also very aware of how many of our students actually actively negotiate multiple literacy repertoires in their writing. Yet, they are also very aware that most, if not all, scholarly works that address these issues, including those mentioned here, despite any claims supporting different literacy practices, are written in prose that align with academic discourse. Even this one. This brings me back to the consultants' question about hypocrisy.

Methodology and Methods

Invested in Practitioner Inquiry as I am, pursuing the question posed by my consultants through empirical research is a natural direction. Moreover, the opportunity to work in NUIG's Academic Writing Centre provided a unique opportunity to conduct the same study at two different sites. I drew on the basic tenets of Practitioner Inquiry as laid out in the preceding chapters, including those that attend to issues of collaboration and the social construction of knowledge, to guide the research design. First, in both locations, I was a practitioner conducting research in the site of practice. At UHM, I had been the writing center director for six years, and although my time at NUIG was limited to one semester, I was there to assist in the direction of the center and with the training of consultants. Obviously, the truncated time in

Ireland presented its own set of challenges. Particularly, I was mindful of the relative power my positionality as a visiting scholar afforded me in relation to the consultants, and the limitations presented by the research context, specifically in terms of mediating that power. Additionally, I could not assume the dynamic in my home center would be the same at NUIG's center. I was unsure whether I could establish rapport quickly enough with the NUIG consultants for them to feel comfortable being candid with me about their writing center work. Years of working closely with my home center consultants had reinforced their agency over our center and their work; over the years, they had demonstrated to me time and again that they were comfortable coming to me with questions, issues, and ideas, as is evident in the question about the conflict between teaching academic discourse and supporting students' multiple literacy repertoires, the subject under study here. This important work of building camaraderie among us was accomplished over time through practices informed by Practitioner Inquiry, but not solely through research, and I knew I would need to begin similarly in my new location to come close to building the same relationships.

I am not sure if it is because of our comparable contexts, the committed and welcoming NUIG director, with whom I share many core values in approaches to our work, or if it is that writing centers generally attract committed and conscientious students, who, by the nature of their work, are also welcoming—but it is likely a combination of these variables that helped with the rapport-building. However, I knew that even if my efforts to establish positive and reciprocal working relationships were successful, the constraints imposed by my limited time in Ireland would impact the ways collaboration could be achieved. So, I focused on aspects of collaboration I could attend to, with identifying how the consultants at NUIG might benefit from our work together being a primary concern. I quickly fell into familiar practices—I met with the consultants regularly, talked with them about their academic goals, collaborated with them on writing center projects, and participated in their training. I also worked with several consultants on scholarship and program applications. Implementing practices that emphasized collaboration and respect for the knowledge and expertise research participants bring, two main theories guiding this model of Practitioner Inquiry, were begun weeks before I began collecting data. Although with just four months I knew I would always remain an outsider, I was lucky enough to be the recipient of NUIG's consultants' generosity in sharing their knowledge.

One of the ways this project most obviously manifests collaboration is in the articulation of the overarching research problem. Following John Creswell's (2009) model, I began with the research problem the consultants had identified—the ethical disjuncture between claims to support varied literacy repertoires and guiding students in the reproduction of academic discourse that often masks those repertoires—which ensured that the project was also of import to them. As I have told my consultants, I do not have a good answer to this question, but I am less interested in claiming or disproving us hypocrites than I am in identifying ethical practices that reaffirm our ideals about access and inclusivity by supporting students' literacy practices, and, at the same time, support acquisition of skills that can aid in succeeding in academia. I see the consultants we work with as the next generation—receiving the proverbial baton so to speak, and it is their energy, ideals, and values that will inform our future academic trajectories. I also know from experience working with many of my consultants in administrative positions, they have innovative ideas about writing and working with writers. I thus decided that the consultants themselves were the best sources of information to respond to my/our research problem. Asking consultants whether they think we are hypocrites or not, however, seemed reductive, and while it might provide a "yes" or "no" to the question, it would not attend to the pragmatics of the issue—what should be done, how do we do it, and/or what is preventing us from doing it. I thus identified the following two central research questions:

1   Should multiple literacy repertoires be accounted for in academic discourse? Why or why not?
2   As writing center practitioners, can we/how do we support students' multiple literacy repertoires when producing academic writing?

These research questions provided the basis for the four interview questions:

1   What do you think about [NUIG or UH] being a bilingual institution? What does that mean for students? Do you have any thoughts on what that means for learning and writing in school?
2   Is there an ideal way for multiple languages/literacies to coexist and be used in public places?
3   Should multiliteracies (i.e., different languages and ways of using those languages, including in making arguments) be accounted for in academic writing/discourses? What would/should that look like?

4   Should we, and, if so, how do we honor all students' literacy practices as writing center practitioners? In other words, is it possible to support students writing for the academy, and, at the same time, encourage them to represent their linguistic identity in their writing? Why or why not?

I worked with two interview cohorts: 14 writing center consultants from the UHM writing center, and four writing center consultants from the NUIG Academic Writing Centre. The disparity in number of respondents between the two cohorts is mostly a function of the number of consultants that work in the respective centers—at UHM, we usually have between 18 and 24 consultants every semester, whereas NUIG's Academic Writing Centre usually has between six and seven consultants. It is also partially a function of the number of consultants who consented to participate in the study and the number of interviews/surveys I was able to conduct in the allotted time. The ratio of the two cohorts in terms of representation is approximately 22% NUIG/78% UHM. I treat the collective responses by each cohort as its own data set; thus, I worked with two data sets, with the distinguishing characteristic being the location of the respective writing centers. I conducted all interviews between February 9 and March 7, 2019, while I was in Ireland. All interviews with NUIG consultants were conducted face-to-face, recorded, and later transcribed. The UHM consultant cohort responded to a secure online questionnaire featuring the same interview questions.

The model of Practitioner Inquiry articulated in this book does not dictate every approach in the research process; rather, practitioners should identify those approaches most suitable for their research context. In this study, I approached the qualitative analysis of the data using content analysis as explained by Bruce Berg (2001) working at the element of "theme" (p. 246). Berg explains content analysis as appropriate for "artifacts of social communication," including transcribed interviews and other written communication (p. 240). Berg (2001) notes that content analysis can solely represent qualitative data but is strengthened when combined with quantitative representation. Thus, as Berg (2009) recommends for quantitative representation, I quantify the "specific frequencies of relevant categories" (p. 242) from each cohort as well as the combined totals. Beginning with open coding following Creswell's (2009) process, I first identified 101 data points, direct quotations taken from both cohort's responses. After repeating the open coding process multiple times, 84 data points were categorized into three themes (which I discuss in the next section), with approximately 26% of the data points coming from the NUIG cohort, and 74% from the UHM cohort, which approximates the 22/78% makeup of the cohorts.

Data and Analysis

The interview questions yielded responses that coalesced around three themes: benefits of incorporating multiliteracy repertoires into academic discourse, the challenges of including multiliteracy repertoires, and how they as writing center practitioners support multiliteracy repertoires. Table 4.1 represents the breakdown of responses categorized under each of these themes.

While every respondent from both cohorts answered that they were in favor of including multiple literacy repertoires in academic discourse (Research Question 1), the discussions that emerged from those statements in terms of why it is important proved to be much more provocative. Twenty-five responses were coded under the theme "Benefits of Multiliteracy Repertoires in Academic Discourse." Several members of both cohorts couched their responses as social justice, correlating the marginalization of certain language practices as exclusionary and potentially denying individual's experiences:

> I think that we should be able to create a space where everyone is welcome no matter how or what or like what's going on, what language you speak, how they look like. It just doesn't matter because everyone's experiences and everyone's learning journeys are equally important.
> (NUIG Consultant)

Table 4.1 Distribution of Data Points across Themes by Cohort

	Total Responses (Data Points)	Benefits of Multiliteracy Repertoires in Academic Discourse	Challenges of Including Multiliteracy Repertoires	How Writing Center Practitioners Support Multiliteracy Repertoires
NUIG cohort	22 (26%)	6 (24%)	13 (32%)	3 (17%)
UHM cohort	62 (74%)	19 (76%)	28 (68%)	15 (83%)
Total	84	25	41	18

> I think that every person is *entitled* to use whatever language is most comfortable to them [emphasis added].
>
> (UHM Consultant)

The consultants did not only focus on how privileging academic discourse disenfranchised certain students, but also pointed to the benefits of active inclusion of translanguaging for the larger learning environment:

> I think that language shapes our world in a way. And so, I think that knowing that you're free to kind of communicate and express yourself in the language that you feel is the best one for you to do so, it's going to enhance the learning experience in so many ways.
>
> (NUIG Consultant)

An UHM consultant expanded to directly address the implications for students on the audience end of inclusionary practices:

> Every language deserves the opportunity to be used and taught, not for the language itself, but for the people who can benefit from going just a little outside their own box for a minute. Just allowing students the opportunity to discern between texts of unfamiliar languages offers opportunity for their own growth.

In addition to the incorporation of multiple languages being democratizing in that a wider range of students would feel that their ways of communicating are not inferior to those privileged in the academy, consultants from both cohorts recognized the potential of inclusionary language practices to transform the educational experience. Consultants reflected on the ways translanguaging in academia could result in a more "holistic way of thinking" (NUIG Consultant) and "new way[s] of discovering and encountering ideas and making connections" (NUIG Consultant). Some consultants suggested translanguaging could have a broader impact on teaching of writing in general, asserting it could help "writing/discourse in the classroom to grow rather than stagnate" (UHM Consultant), and "expand or reinvent how writing is viewed by many students" (UHM Consultant). At the same time, many also acknowledged that they could not imagine how such practices would manifest in final form, with one NUIG consultant simply stating it would be "messy."

Across almost every set of responses, these laudatory ideas framing translanguaging as social justice and its pedagogical potential moved into speculation about the friction incorporating translanguaging could cause in the face of academic conventions and norms. These responses address Research Question 2 in that they highlight the obstacles that inclusion of multiple repertoires must attend to when deciding how to go about such work. These comments were coded under the theme "Challenges of Including Multiliteracy Repertoires," which encompasses 41 data points. Some of the critiques of academic norms were subtle, with one UHM consultant writing, "by going beyond the traditional form of academic writing and placing more importance on meaning, I feel it can become possible to account for multiliteracies in academic writing/discourse," suggesting the focus on form has limiting effects on the possibilities for meaning-making. Another UHM consultant highlighted the institutional role in legitimating translanguaging, while also indirectly drawing attention to the narrow purview of current norms: "If multiple languages are to co-exist, the institutional understanding of what languages are privileged and valued must dramatically change." However, as the consultants moved to talking about their tutoring experiences in relation to these challenges, more pointed conflicts emerged.

Responses from both cohorts pointed to the real impact current institutional norms have on students for whom translanguaging is not something that they can turn on and off at will to meet the demands of writing academic discourse. Many of the consultants noted that students who do not/cannot adhere to academic discourse conventions— even when there is nothing overtly "wrong" with the writing— face repercussions in the form of bad grades or other assessments. Some of the responses addressed how language differences can manifest in misunderstanding of expectations: "These differences in language and use of languages can often create conflict between what the instructor has asked and how the student interprets and responds to the assignment" (UHM consultant). Others acknowledged that writing outside of the expected academic norms has direct consequences in terms of academic success. When describing working with a student whose first language is not English, a NUIG consultant stated, "I need to try to help them understand the English way of writing commas, because I know that in this system in NUIG, they'd be penalized for using that... particular phraseology." A UHM consultant similarly drew from experiences working with Japanese students who are used to different academic genres, noting, "In the US, making one's opinion and supporting it with evidence is highly valued and expected, so if Japanese students write such essays/construct such arguments [using accepted Japanese norms], they will receive low grades."

Despite their own ideas about supporting inclusionary linguistic practices, consultants from both cohorts are well aware that forms not aligned with conventional academic discourse are not often seen as different, but as inferior. A NUIG consultant framed this marginalization in a discussion of rigor: "I think the implication of that is [there is] extra rigor [in writing Academic Discourse compared to other languages], which I don't necessarily hold to be true." A UHM consultant similarly reflected, "I feel that there is a perception within institutions that certain types of writing that deviate from academic writing in its traditional form is somehow inferior and thus not as acceptable." References like these to the consequences of translanguaging in writing for school in the data are numerous and detailed, with many specifically noting that the "problems" identified in such writing can be arbitrary. For example, a NUIG consultant reflected on their experience working with a student who used "language ... that for me is fresh and exciting, but...can be torn apart by an academic."

This conflict between seeing translanguaging as democratizing yet marginalized in the acadamy, especially when it comes to grades, is not necessarily surprising, and, in many ways, mirror claims made in the scholarship. As noted earlier, Horner et al. (2011) frame a translingual approach to teaching writing as social justice, articulating such an approach as aligning with the Conference on College Composition and Communications' statement "Students' Rights to Their own Language" that "oppose[s] the common, though inaccurate, view that varieties of English other than those recognized as 'standard' are defective. It also opposed the view, just as inaccurate, that speakers of these varieties are themselves somehow substandard" (p. 304). Horner et al. (2011) go on to outline approaches that create space for translingual writing without compromising rigor and, similar to what the consultants noted, assert that engaging translingual practices has the potential to expand opportunities for meaning making.

Despite that many scholars in Composition Studies are working to incorporate translingual approaches, many others have identified the same problems the consultants did in terms of marginalization and assessment consequences. Canagarajah (2011) notes how employing multiple linguistic forms is often perceived as inferior: "Multilinguals users' linguistic variations are treated as marking their nonstandard or deficient usage, resulting from 'interference' from the other languages in their repertoire" (pp. 2–3). And like the responses that correlate a lack of mastery over academic discourse with compromised success, Jerry Won Lee (2016) notes, "Classroom grading practices have been closely connected to an unchallenged, dominant discursive standard in writing classrooms and programs" (p. 175). Thus, in terms of the data from this study coded under both "Benefits of Multiliteracy Repertoires in Academic Discourse" and "Challenges of Including Multiliteracy Repertoires," the consultants' responses can be mapped onto the scholarship conversations.

However, the consultants' responses went beyond claims that align with the politics of translanguaging expressed in the literature to highlight the conflicts it creates in their work as tutors, a topic much less discussed in our scholarship. Two NUIG consultants framed the conflict as a juxtaposition between supporting student's individual communicative practices and the student's goals of succeeding in the academy: "I think as tutors… [we need to mediate] how far away we can encourage a student to do what they feel like doing because we're too scared of grades constantly";

> I think that it's just really difficult when students come here [to the center]…to have that balance, to be inclusive, to respect their ideas, their identities, their language, and to kind of fit it into the academic world to produce a paper that respects all of us.

Again, UHM consultants represented similar attitudes: "I do feel that perhaps this goal of supporting students' identities and their voices may contradict with our expectations of teaching academic writing"; and,

> [Translanguaging] can present a bit of a tension, because as a reader I want to nurture and value their [student writer's] voice and perspective without boxing it into the parameters set by academia, whereas, as a consultant, I know that this student wants to receive a good grade in their course, which is sometimes contingent upon how well they enact the accepted academic discourse.

One UHM consultant invoked the two main variables to describe the conflict succinctly: "As a writing consultant, I always struggled with how we navigate between supporting students' writing for the academy without erasing their voices and their cultures." "Difficulty." "Contradict." "Tension." "Struggle." All words the consultants used to describe what it means for them to negotiate these competing goals. Writing center literature does provide a good deal of direction in terms of best practices for supporting writers as they mediate their translingual practices with the expectations of their professors/courses, and many of these practices were specifically mentioned by the consultants (which I will discuss next). But there is not much, if any, scholarship that attends to the inner turmoil our consultants negotiate when they try to support writers through this process, or despite any movement to support translanguaging, what it means that, as one NUIG consultant observed, the fundamental message still is, "we should all work towards the same goal of writing in Standard academic [discourse]..... that should be the ultimate goal."

Finally, 18 responses were coded under the theme, "How Writing Center Practitioners Support Multiliteracy Repertoires," which also attends to Research Question 2. It is in these responses that I see the consultants' professionalization as writing center practitioners and their commitment to our work and values. The consultants talked about how important it is to make writers feel "intellectually safe," by encouraging them and being supportive. They mentioned specific practices like listening, asking questions, addressing the writers' priorities and concerns, and working on higher order concerns—all of which should be recognizable to those of us familiar with writing center's best practices. Consultants from both cohorts noted how writing centers are ideally positioned for this work despite the complications that it brings. Moreover, their responses point to the many ways they push through any inner conflicts they may be feeling in terms of negotiating the tensions between democratizing language use in academia and adhering to academic norms and conventions by relying on their training. And, quite remarkably, the two cohorts, working on opposite sides of the planet in two very different in situations, seemed to have embraced very similar ideals of how to perform this work and the role centers play in supporting writers' multiple linguistic identities.

Discussion and Recommendations

In the context of this book, the strength of this study is twofold.

First, as an example of Practitioner Inquiry, it demonstrates how a single study can be conducted across two sites. The coalescence of the responses around unified themes by two distinct cohorts representing different geographic and sociopolitical contexts is worth comment. That consultants trained on two continents, by two different directors, in institutions with very different histories of teaching writing, gave strikingly similar responses tells us so much about what we share. Equally important, in terms of one of the foci of this book, it complicates what it means to enact collaboration. Saying the study has collaborative aspects is accurate, but that does not tell the whole story. It is collaborative in that the research problem was identified collaboratively and that the initiators of that problem/question participated in answering it through their responses to online and face-to-face interviews. However, the overall design—the decision to conduct interviews, the collection and coding of the data, and the final analysis—was not collaborative in a tangible way. This assessment of collaboration does not detract from what is collaborative about the study, but rather creates a critical lens as to the extent of the collaboration—I am not claiming collaboration infused every part of this study, but I am claiming that the ways in which collaboration was engendered took the study in a powerful, and under-examined direction (on my own, I may never have pursued the problem/question under examination here).

This brings me to the second strength of the study: its findings. Surely, the statements consultants provided that align with current scholarship in terms of translanguaging being democratizing and potentially having positive pedagogical implications point to potential for further study to determine how consultants' attitudes mirror the scholarship and move beyond it. A more concerning finding is the conflict our consultants negotiate as they juggle what they see as the mandates of the job: supporting each individual writer and their way of knowing, being, and communicating while ensuring they have the tools to succeed in academia, which is commonly understood as conforming to academic writing conventions. Whatever the position our individual centers take on translanguaging, this study tells me I need to do a better job in providing guidance to my consultants to specifically address how to negotiate this conflict. Many of the recent articles on translanguaging and translingual approaches to writing give us strategies and ideas for ways to incorporate practices in our classrooms, or how to engage with translanguaging in the writing process. In consideration of the consultants' responses, however, that is not enough. Those of us in positions with more relative cultural capital when compared to that of our consultants should be addressing how our support for translanguaging is realized or problematized beyond our own classrooms because our consultants do not have the luxury of defining their own contexts of influence. They are working with writers from across our campuses who are confronted with different paradigms for assessment, with many of their learning environments privileging academic discourse at the expense of other kinds of writing. Writing center practitioners have always negotiated the tensions between our ideals and the often exclusionary expectations of the academy—we have embraced that liminal space. This study calls for this kind of work once again—to openly engage with the tensions so we can lay bare the politics of language use ensconced when we advocate for multiple literacy repertoires and the identities they represent at the same time we adhere to the conventions of academic discourse in our own work.

Furthering this project would necessitate adding another cohort. A third group of consultants could add a geographic component to the responses, but a cohort that includes writing center directors and/or writing teachers might prove more beneficial in actually attending to the original problem of aligning our practices to our ideals of inclusivity. Getting feedback from an administrator/teacher cohort could move this project toward identifying strategies to mitigate the tensions our consultants have identified that they negotiate in these efforts. While the practices the consultants noted that they employ, such as listening, asking questions, and honoring the writer's concerns and priorities, are noted best practices, they are generally advocated for working with all writers. The findings of this study suggest we need to attend to the particulars of what it means to support multiliteracy practices by addressing what it can and should look like in writing. As a first step, we can begin by answering questions such as the following: Who are we writing for when we produce writing in the academy? Is our audience confined to those who are conveyers of academic discourse? Are there limits to supporting multiliteracy practices in terms of producing academic discourse? Should evidences of translingual writing be constrained to in-process writing but eliminated in final products? How can multiliteracy repertoires in a final product look? Would it resemble practices I have used in this book that follow Kanaka Maoli scholars who include words and concepts in ʻōlelo Hawaiʻi? Or can it even go further? Whether we as individuals support incorporating multiliteracy repertoires into academic discourse or not, I encourage those of us with relative cultural capital in our institutions to move beyond identifying our ideals to articulating how they manifest in practice and acknowledging the implications of our positions for ourselves and the writers we work with.

Notes

1 For a more detailed account of language politics in Hawaiʻi as a result of the overthrow and subsequent plantation system, see Larry Kimura's (1983) "Native Hawaiian Culture."

2 I use Standard English here, fully acknowledging that there is no standard; I use this term because it is a phrase commonly used in Hawai'i to refer to American English (also not a uniform language).
3 For more information on efforts at language revitalization in Ireland, see the Conradh na Gaeilge website, https://www.cnag.ie/ga/eolas/anghaeilge/stair-chonradh-na-gaeilge.html
4 See Chapter 2 for a fuller discussion of this phenomenon in relation to 'ōlelo Hawai'i.
5 In conversations with colleagues across the USA, it seems that many of us are experiencing increasing numbers of students who speak languages other than, or in addition to, English in our classrooms and centers. Mentions of these dynamics are so common, I was quite surprised when I could not find any hard data on how many languages are represented by college students in the USA, or even at my own institution. I learned that language demographics is often not tracked. With a little more investigation, I learned not tracking language use plays a role in reproducing the marginalization of students who are often labeled as remedial because their lack of proficiency in speaking and/or writing Standard English is not recognized as relating to language learning.

References

Anzaldua, G. (1987). *Borderlands/La Frontera: The new mestiza* (1st ed.). San Francisco, CA: Spinsters/Aunt Lute.
Berg, B. (2001). *Qualitative research methods for the social sciences* (4th ed.). Needham Heights, MA: Allyn & Bacon.
Bromley, P., Northway, K., & Schonberg, E. (2019). From the Editors. *Writing Center Journal, 37*(2), 11–14.
Canagarajah, S. (2011). Translanguaging in the classroom: Emerging issues for research and pedagogy. *Applied Linguistics Review, 2*, 1–28.
Creswell, J. (2009). *Research design: Qualitative, quantitative, and mixed methods approaches*. Thousand Oaks, CA: Sage Publications.
DiPardo, A. (1992). "Whispers of coming and going": Lessons from Fannie. *The Writing Center Journal, 12*(2), 125–144.
Gilyard, K. (2016). The rhetoric of translingualism. *College English, Special Issue: Translingual Work in Composition, 78*(3), 284–289.
Horner, B., Lu, M., Royster, J., & Trimbur, J. (2011). Language difference in writing: Toward a translingual approach. *College English, 73*(3), 303–321.
Kimura, L. (1983). "Native Hawaiian culture." In United States Native Hawaiian Study Commission (Ed.), *Report on the culture, needs and concerns of native Hawaiians pursuant to Public Law 96-565, Title III* (pp. 173–224). Washington, DC: The Commission.
Lee, J. W. (2016). Beyond translingual writing. *College English, 70*(2), 174–195.
Lu, M. Z., & Horner, B. (2016). Introduction: Translingual work. *College English, Special Issue: Translingual Work in Composition, 78*(3), 207–218.
Lyons, S. R. (2009). The fine art of fencing: Nationalism, hybridity, and the search for a Native American writing pedagogy. *JAC, 29*(1–2), 77–105.

Young, V. A., Barrett, R., Young-Rivera, Y., & Lovejoy, K. B. (2014). *Other people's English: Code-meshing, code-switching, and African American literacy.* New York, NY: Teachers College Press.

Young, V. A., Martinez, A. Y., & Naviaux, J. A. (2011). Introduction: Code-meshing as world English. In V. A. Young, & A. Y. Martinez (Eds.), *Code-meshing as world English: Pedagogy, policy, and performance* (pp. xix–xxxi). Urbana, IL: NCTE.

Epilogue
A Practitioner's Final Thoughts

Writing centers are built on principles of social justice. At the very core of our work with writers are issues of access, agency, and inclusivity, and practices that promote these ideals permeate through everything we do. The issues of access we negotiate are not limited to our efforts to support writers; we have also had to fight for recognition and legitimation of the services we provide, the centers we work in, and the people who work in them. Articulating our centers as pedagogical sites that support research—the mantra I espouse—captures one of the ways we have legitimated our work in academia. Drawing attention to the multidirectional teaching involved in tutoring writing—from training consultants, to consultant-writer interactions, to mentoring consultants in administration—has helped reframe and complicate the service centers provide so they are better understood as teaching endeavors. And through our research, we have not only codified our practices but also revealed the rich environments writing centers provide for explorations into possibilities for equity and democratization. The recent aggressive moves in the scholarship to embrace empirical research only further these ideals, as through empirical study we legitimate practices designed to achieve access, agency, and inclusivity by demonstrating the tangible impacts these approaches have on students, both the writers who visit our centers and those who work in them.

I have strived for my own work to contribute to these efforts. Like so many others have reflected, my journey into this field began with me tutoring, and I was hooked by those magical moments when I realized that through this work, I could be an ally to writers who thought their only place in academia is on the periphery. At the same time, every day I came to work I learned something, and in small and large ways, I was motivated to find new and innovative ways to support writers, as they, knowingly or not, inspired my academic journey. As I moved into administration, I noticed similar interactions between me as the director and the consultants I worked with—dynamic multidirectional learning in an environment that persistently pushes us to respond to the obstacles students face as they try to exercise their agency over their access. The work we do is political; there is no escaping it. But I suspect that many writing center practitioners embrace our political positioning. As I write this, an open letter to the board of the International Writing Center Association, our field's representative organization, is circulating, calling for statements in support of the Black Lives Matter movement and international students being affected by current immigration policies. Such efforts are just one more indication of the many ways practitioners constantly work to operationalize the values writing centers are founded on.

The model of Practitioner Inquiry I have presented in this volume foregrounds the practitioner so as to lay bare these values guiding our work. And, as teaching, service, and research are not separate endeavors for the practitioner working in such contexts, the model also combines principles to guide ethical practices in all three. In the theory of collaboration presented in Chapter 2, I have identified tenets that, when adopted holistically, can infuse all our endeavors with an ethical consciousness. I looked to Indigenous concepts, specifically Kanaka Maoli, precisely because their approaches are grounded in a holism that engenders an awareness that the implications of our interactions go beyond the engaged individuals and extend to our communities, the places we live, and the lands we live on. Kanaka Maoli approaches inform an interdependence among rights, privileges, and responsibility—these ideas that are conceived of separately in a Western frame are conceptualized in a single encompassing concept, kuleana. Combined with the emphasis on reciprocity and respect, adapting these approaches in our enactments of collaboration engenders a critical reflective practice that can equip practitioners in their negotiation of the webs of concerns and interests we encounter in our work.

The examination into application of the tenets for collaboration is designed to accomplish several goals: (1) demonstrate how Practitioner Inquiry can guide practice, (2) investigate the efficacy of an approach guided by Practitioner Inquiry in terms of achieving collaboration and its effect on consultants' professionalization, (3) demonstrate how Practitioner Inquiry can guide research, and (4) promote an understanding of collaboration as more complicated than an all or nothing endeavor. I see this work too as aligned with social justice as examinations that place collaboration on a continuum challenge our assumptions about what collaborative interactions achieve. In this

A Practitioner's Final Thoughts 121

case, the data indicate that collaborative practices informed by the tenets laid out in Chapter 2 do correlate to increased consultant professionalization; however, the data also illustrate that collaboration is much more complicated than often presented in the literature—it can be achieved to varying degrees. Understanding these kinds of limitations prompts increased critical engagement in terms of what we claim about our collaborative practices.

The final study employing Practitioner Inquiry to investigate how consultants negotiate supporting writers' multiple linguistic repertoires with producing academic writing is ultimately an examination of the politics of language use in the academy, again a social justice issue.[1] Using a critical lens guided by the tenets of collaboration to assess the design of the study exposes exactly where collaboration was realized and where it was not. My goal is that in capturing both presence and absence, I provide another example of what it means to critically examine our claims of collaboration. That kind of reflection makes us more accountable and identifies areas where we may need to focus more if we are to truly live up to our ideals. The study itself provides important insights into guidance our consultants may need as they endeavor to negotiate the conflicts between democratizing ideals surrounding linguistic inclusivity and hierarchical structures that reinforce gatekeeping in the academy. These findings also suggest that those of us in relative positions of power as administrators may need to examine how we mediate these same tensions and recognize the importance of acknowledging the conflicts we encounter in these negotiations.

Collectively, the work presented in this book is my response to the position that Practitioner Inquiry is aligned with informal studies that are subjected to merely holding potential to inform more rigorous research. I have presented a detailed model with corresponding studies that demonstrate systematicity and rigor. But the model does more than this—it emphasizes the importance of identifying our methodologies, the theoretical grounding that informs the approaches to our work, the values we foreground, and the ethics we try to engender. Methodologies are often not included in traditional research designs, such as those employed in disciplines like the sciences that downplay social implications in the research process. Detailing our methodologies lays our politics bare, and, in its ability to make transparent the values that guide our work, also has the potential to further solidify the inherency of social justice to our work.

Right now, as I finish writing this book, a devastating pandemic is raging across the world—with the US suffering catastrophically.

At the same time, the US is also experiencing a long overdue reckoning with its racist history and ongoing intercommunal and institutionalized racism. Conversations on academic Listservs are focused on how we safely open up our schools and provide services to our students. More than ever, I am feeling the need to embrace our liminal position and use it to get into "good trouble"—trouble that confronts the racism that disenfranchises black and brown students and colleagues, trouble that affirms DACA (Deferred Action for Childhood Arrivals) students, trouble that acknowledges our students do not all go home to the same privileges and responsibilities. I am an advocate of our field's commitment to systematic rigorous empirical research, not only for the important knowledge it yields but also for the way it forces those who have traditionally marginalized support services to take notice. Such research has given us valuable tools for understanding the obstacles our own positionality presents in our efforts to support writers from various backgrounds and identities. But I would also argue that going forward, it is instrumental to work within a frame that demands an accounting of the ways in which our work does or does not attend to our values. Centering the practitioner and articulating our methodologies—features embedded in the Practitioner Inquiry model I have presented—give us a frame for grounding our work in these values and then critically reflecting on them so that transparency becomes an elemental feature of how we do social justice.

Note

1 Vershawn Ashanti Young, Chair of the 2020 Conference on College Composition and Communication (CCCC), announced just this week (August 3, 2020), CCCC's formal adoption of a Position Statement on Black Linguistic Justice, pointing to the currency of such issues in Composition and Rhetoric more generally.

Index

Note: **Bold** page numbers refer to tables; *italic* page numbers refer to figures and page numbers followed by "n" denote endnotes.

academic inferiority 2
academic preparedness 4
academic writing 107, 111–113, 115, 121
accountability 50
administration 20, 76, 77, 91, 120
Affective Coding Method 89
agency 1, 2, 14, 20, 35, 37, 40, 62, 89
American English 56, 117n2
American literacy practices 103
Anzaldua, Gloria 99, 102
Assistant Director 83, 85, 87
authors group validity 64
awareness 35, 37, 44

Babcock, Rebecca Day 15, 18
Barnes, Jeffrey 68, 69
Berg, Bruce 68, 88, 108
Black Lives Matter movement 120
British colonization 100
Brown, Marie Alohalani 45
Bruffee, Kenneth 28, 32, 34, 36, 37, 78, 85

Canagarajah, Suresh 101, 112
catalytic validity 65
central research question 79
classroom grading practices 112–113
client relations 77
Cochran-Smith, Marilyn 8, 10, 11, 22n3, 39, 57, 59–62, 64–68, 83
code-switching 102

collaboration theory 3, 19, 25, 28; assessment of 115; concept of 29; constructing knowledge 39; definition of 33; dialogic 35, 36; discussions of 34; dominant theories on 34; employing 79; ethical approaches 29; hierarchical 35; ideal goal of 49; importance of 29; intellectual and ethical potential of 28; and social construction of knowledge 9; structure and objective of 48; theoretical treatments of 34; work environment 80; in writing studies 32–40
colonization, impacts of 98
commonalities 57–60
communication 102
community participation 44
competence 79
CompPile 32
conceptual inquiry 2
Conference on College Composition and Communication (CCCC) 12, 112, 122n1
consultants 110; knowledge 83, 86; methodology 78–81; NUIG consultants 111, 112, 114; opportunities for 86; pedagogical space for 77; professional development 92; professionalization 79, 81–87; UHM consultants 111–113;

workshop project 86; *vs.* writer 38; and writer interactions 119
conversation analysis 63
corpus-driven analysis 63
Creswell, John 79, 80, 89, 107, 108

DACA (Deferred Action for Childhood Arrivals) 122
data-based inquiry 13
data-based research 6
democratic social theory 8
democratic validity 65
Denny, Harry 1
dialectic exchange 63, 72
dialogic mode 37
dialogic validity 65
DiPardo, Anne 104
director-consultant work relationship 76, 78–79
discourse: "abnormal" 34; analysis 63; "normal" 34
discourse community 34
Driscoll, Dana 7, 14, 18, 22n6, 61, 63
Du Bois, John W. 11
Duffy, William 33, 34

Early Teacher Research projects 7
Ede, Lisa 28, 35–37, 39
education 3, 39; policies 25; system 25; and writing center studies **58**
empiricism 4; investigation 2, 4, 79; research model 12–16, 70–72
end-of-semester evaluations 94
English 43, 44, 52n3, 81, 99; marginalization of 102
equality concepts 42
equity concepts 42
ethical: collaboration 44; disjuncture 107; interactions 44; and support inclusivity 3
ethnography 64
EuroAmerican norms 55
Euro-Western settlers/researchers 25; societies 29

feminist theory 11, 37
First Year Writing (FYW) 86

Geertz, Clifford 64
generalizability 60, 64, 65–66, 68, 69

generosity 43, 48
Gillam, Alice 17, 18
Gillespie, Paula 13, 14, 76, 77, 78, 95n1
Gilyard, Keith 104
Glaser, Barney 56
Goodyear-Kaʻōpua, Noelani 44, 45
Google Scholar 17
Goswami, Dixie 7
grounded theory 56

Harding, Sandra 2, 62
Haswell, Richard 12–15, 61
Hawaiʻi 3, 25, 40, 46, 73n1, 98; language politics 101; translingual approaches 100
Hawaiʻi Creole 55; *see also* Pidgin
Hawaiian kingdom 98
higher education 60
hoʻomanawanui, kuʻuloha 44
Horner, Bruce 104, 112
Huberman, Michael 80
Hughes, Bradley 76, 77, 78, 95n1
hybrid language approaches 104

inclusivity 4, 5, 11, 119
"independent" code 89
Indigenous: approaches 5; collaborative practices 30; language 25; nations 40; Native people 25; peoples 40; scholars 67; social and governmental systems 27; studies scholarship 30; theories 4
individualism 29, 47
informal mode of inquiry 17
innovations 27, 82
inquiry 6, 7, 76; informal mode of 17; professionalization 76; stance 57
integrity 7
intellectual engagement 27
intellectual heritage 32
International Writing Center Association 120
investment category 92
in vivo groupings 89, **90**
Ireland 100, 106
Isaacs, Emily 78

Jackson, Rebecca 82
Jordan, Kerri 14, 18, 57, 59, 61–68

Index

Kail, Harvey 76, 77, 78, 95n1
Kanaka Maoli (Hawaiian) 11, 25, 29, 30, 32, 40, 41, 46, 55, 98, 99, 116, 120
Kimura, Larry 43
Kinkead, Joyce 15
Kirsch, Geza 37, 38
knowledge 27, 79, 83; making 67; social construction of 9, 84, 86; theory 84; transmission 8
Kolba, Ellen 78

language: community 93; dynamics 99; groups 4; politics 101, 116
Lanikai Canoe Club 42
learning 91
Lee, Jerry Won 112
liaison 85
Liggett, Sarah 14, 18, 57, 59, 61–68
limitations 57, 60–66
linguistic: democracy 103; scholars 22n4, 93
Lu, Min Zhan 104
Lunsford, Andrea 28, 35–37, 39, 51, 60, 84
Lyons, Scott Richard 104
Lytle, Susan 8, 10, 11, 22n3, 39, 57, 59–62, 64–68, 83

McDougall, Brandy Nālani 25, 26, 30, 32
Mackiewicz, Jo 15
McKinney, Jackie Grutsch 15, 17, 82
marginalization 6, 21, 22n9, 29, 47, 102, 109, 112
Martinez, Aja Y. 102
meaning-making process 101
Merriam-Webster 33
methodology 2–3, 16, 56, 62; collaboration as 62; consultants 78–81; definitions of 62; vs. methods 62
methods 2–3; definitions of 62; description of 16; examples of 15; vs. methodology 62
Miles, Matthew 80
moʻokūʻauhau (genealogy) 32
multidirectional collaborative relationship 79, 81
multilingual speakers 4

multilingual students 105
multiple linguistic codes 101

National Council of the Teachers of English (NCTE) 12
National University of Ireland, Galway's (NUIG) 100, 105
"Natives Wanted" 25–26, 30
Naviaux, Julie A. 102
non-dominant languages 69
non-Indigenous backgrounds 32; person 46; students 5
North, Stephen M. 13, 14
NUIG Academic Writing Centre 108

ʻōlelo Hawaiʻi (Hawaiian language) 99, 100
opportunity 105
organization 63

participant-observation 5, 49, 88
pedagogy: approach 1; space 85
Perdue, Sherry Wynn 7, 14, 18, 22n6, 61, 63
Pidgin 98, 102; speakers 4; speaking parents 99
place-based pedagogy 11
power structures 35
practitioner 2, 5, 6, 9, 14, 27–29, 38, 39, 56, **58**, 61, 63, 70, 71, 75, 82, 109; stance 7–12, 16, 25, 47, 48–51, 60, 65, 83
Practitioner Inquiry 4, 6, 7–12; application of 20; categorizations of 17; commonalities 57–60; "common characteristics" of 57; education and writing center studies **58**; vs. empirical research 64; empirical research model 70–72; limitations 57, 60–66; as viable response 16–21; writing center research 18, 66–70; writing center studies 57
Practitioner Inquiry Research Model 66, 69, *70*
Prajean, Kelly 78
Pratt, Mary Louise 28
pre-service teachers working 78
Price, Steve 14, 18, 57, 59, 61–68
professionalism/professionalization 9, 76, 79
"proper" English 98, 99

qualitative: analysis 87, 89, 108; data 19, 64, 67, 69, 87, 108; research 68, 80
quantitative: analysis 87, 92; data 87; representation 108
Queer theory 1, 11

RAD (replicable, aggregable, date-based evidence) research 12–14, 61
reflexive stance 57
reflexivity 63, 64
representation 4
research: concept 27; design 3; model 3, 7; participants 37; robust research model 6; subjects 37; taxonomies 17; teacher paradigm 6; teacher/service 38
responsibility 7, 44, 45, 78
Ritchie, Joy 37, 38

Saldaña, Johnny 89
Scheibman, Joanne 92
scholarship 2, 7, 12, 13, 17, 22n5, 29, 47, 61, 78, 82, 100
settler colonialism 30; American settler colonial culture 46
Silva, Noenoe 43
Silver, Naomi 78
skills, transfer of 78
Smith, Linda Tuhiwai 45–46
social justice 102, 103, 109–112, 119
social turn 28
specialized knowledge 79
specific analytical frameworks 16
sponsorship 12
Standard English 98, 102, 104, 117n2
Stenhouse, Lawrence 7
Stillman, Peter 7
Strauss, Anslem 56
student: consultants 79, 81; empowerment 84; writing 4
success, models for 47
summer internship 78
support: and collaboration categories 92, 94; data-based research 6; empirical research 15; LBTQIA students 11; RAD research 14; translingual literacy practices 20; writing center practitioners 19
systematic investigation 63, 65
systematicity 60, 64, 65, 68, 71, 72

teacher-director 79, 81
teacher-research 56
Teacher Research movement 7
Teaching Composition course 81
theme element of 108
thick description concept 64
Thonus, Terese 15, 18
top-down knowledge dissemination 8
training 91, 92
transferability 68, 69, 71, 77
translanguaging (code-meshing) 103, 104, 110, 112
translingual approaches 100, 104, 105, 112; scholarly positions on 101
transparency 83
Trask, Haunani Kay 30–32, 45
triangulation 68, 71, 72, 87
Trimbur, John 28, 34–36, 37
tutoring environment 78

United States 4, 25; collaborative voice 30; educational system 25; English, dominance of 99; individualism 47
Universal Design Learning 11, 18
University of Hawai'i at Mānoa (UHM) 98, 105, 108, 110, 111

validity 71, 72
Vaughan, Mehana 44

Welsch, Kathleen 77, 78
Western contexts 32
workload 83
workshops 86; Coordinator 87; project 86; template 86
writing center 4: administrators 38; "center for writers" 82; conceptions of 60; critical assessment of 14; director 4, 47, 56, 81, 116; pedagogy 57, 60, 95; political liminality of 14; practice 1; practitioners 3, 15, 28, 63, 64, 67, 71, 76, 109, 114; rapid growth of 13; research 14, 66–70; scholars 17, 18; scholarship 5, 61, 77, 105; services, beyond tutoring 82; studies 2, 3, 5, 13, 57, 77; UHM writing center 108; work 13

Young, V. A. 102, 122n1